I0407471

CANNABIS SENSE 2015

WHY THE UNITED STATES NEEDS TO

LEGALIZE MARIJUANA NOW

Derek Williams, M.S.

Cannabis Sense 2015: Why the United States Needs to Legalize Marijuana Now

Copyright © 2015 by Derek Williams

Published: April 11, 2015

Library of Congress Data:

ISBN-13: 978-1500954376

ISBN-10: 1500954373

Written by Derek Williams

Cover Design by Chris Keal

CANNABIS SENSE 2015

It should be noted that the author is unconnected with any political party, and under no sort of influence public or private, except the influence of reason and principle.

TABLE OF CONTENTS

PREFACE

"Some writers have so confounded society with government, as to leave little or no distinction between them. Whereas they are not only different, but have different origins. Society is produced by our wants, and government by wickedness. The former promotes our happiness positively by uniting our affections, the latter negatively by restraining our vices."

- **Thomas Paine**, *Common Sense* (1776)

Hundreds of informative books have already been written about marijuana. Authors such as Jack Herer (*The Emperor Wears No Clothes*), Ed Rosenthal (*Marijuana Grower's Handbook*) and Greg Green (*The Cannabis Grow Bible*) have already eloquently explained everything you need to know about the history of cannabis, the industrial benefits of hemp and how to grow your own marijuana plants.

This book is different. The mission of *Cannabis Sense 2015* is to logically outline the most compelling reasons why the United States needs to legalize marijuana right now. Every sentence is firmly rooted in science, logic and the truth.

If you love your country and your fellow citizens, I urge you to put aside any preconceived opinions you might have about marijuana and please read this book with an open mind and an open heart.

Thanks for reading and God Bless America.

INTRODUCTION

"I offer nothing more than simple facts, plain arguments, and common sense."

- **Thomas Paine**, *Common Sense* (1776)

Marijuana is the most commonly used term in the United States to describe the flowers and leaves that are produced by the plant *Cannabis sativa*. The words "marijuana" and "cannabis" are used interchangeably throughout this book. Please don't be confused, as both words refer to the same plant.

Cannabis is the most widely used illegal drug in the United States. More than 100 million Americans have tried marijuana at least once, according to the Office of National Drug Control Policy. But when one of these citizens decides to partake in their vice of choice, they risk being arrested and thrown in the slammer.

Each year 750,000 of our fellow citizens are arrested for cannabis possession in America. Right now there are over 40,000 people who are spending their days locked inside cages for cannabis-related offenses. Prosecuting marijuana users presents a huge financial burden for American taxpayers. it costs the American taxpayer $1.6 billion each year to keep these non-violent people trapped behind bars.

Marijuana prohibition in America has been a colossal failure. We have wasted billions of dollars, ruined millions of lives and packed our prisons with people who pose no harm to society.

Our state laws are grossly disparate and totally unfair. While a botanist in Colorado earns a six figure salary growing legal cannabis for his appreciative customers, an eye doctor in Philadelphia gets arrested and thrown in jail for providing his glaucoma patients with medicine harvested from the 25 marijuana plants in his basement.

Legalizing marijuana in the United States in 2015 would result in several immediate benefits. The move would provide a massive boost to our economy, as a multi-billion dollar industry with millions of loyal customers would be created overnight. Local and state governments would collect a giant windfall of much-needed tax dollars. Patients who use marijuana to cope with debilitating conditions like glaucoma or cancer will no longer have to fear being arrested by the police for the unspeakable crime of trying to feel better.

Mexican drug cartels would see their revenues plunge by nearly 50 percent. Police would have more time to devote towards crime prevention and arresting dangerous criminals. The legal system would no longer be clogged up prosecuting people over victimless crimes. Billions of dollars would be saved by eliminating all the police, judicial and correctional resources that were previously dedicated to enforcing marijuana prohibition.

Most importantly, Americans will have freedom. The freedom to choose a safer, less addictive substance than alcohol, tobacco or prescription drugs and use it in whatever way you see fit: medically, scientifically or just for fun.

Common sense demands that all Americans should be allowed the freedom to purchase and consume cannabis in 2015 without the fear of being arrested, fined and thrown in a cage.

With the stroke of a pen, Congress can immediately abolish our nation's outdated laws rooted in 1930's *Reefer Madness* and start over by creating fresh new guidelines that reflect our 21st Century reality.

We cannot continue this ridiculous campaign against nature's most miraculous plant any longer. The United States must take action and legalize marijuana on a federal level in 2015.

CHAPTER 1: LIES, DECEIT AND IGNORANCE

"Not only are moral inhibitions removed and the Ten Commandments abolished in the mind of the confirmed marijuana user, but a positive conviction is added that it is right to steal, commit rape and murder, and that it is actually wrong not to do these horrible things."

- From *On the Trail of Marihuana: The Weed of Madness* (1939) by Earle Albert Rowell & Robert Rowell

The United States government has been lying to its citizens about cannabis for the past 76 years. It doesn't take Sherlock Holmes to see through the bullshit that's been shoveled on top of legitimate scientific and medical research.

Anytime you see a quote from an elected official, government agent or law enforcement officer asserting that marijuana has zero medical value, just follow the money trail and you'll find they are making these false, ignorant statements to maintain the status quo, protect their jobs and provide justification for their existence. They are selfishly putting their own job security ahead of the future of America.

It is unfathomable that any nation would arrest sick people who are seeking pain relief. It is inhumane to deny our fellow citizens safe access to the most effective medicine for their conditions. As you will learn on the following pages, America's tyrannical federal laws against cannabis blatantly defy truth, science and common sense.

America's Narcotics Commissioner was a Racist Lunatic

"Suspicion is the companion of mean souls, and the bane of all good society."

- **Thomas Paine**, *Common Sense* (1776)

In order to understand how marijuana became illegal in the first place, it's essential that you get introduced to a lying scoundrel named Henry J. Anslinger.

Henry J. Anslinger was the highest ranking drug enforcement official in America for 32 consecutive years and he hated cannabis with a passion. President Herbert Hoover appointed Anslinger to a newly created position called "Commissioner of Narcotics" after the Federal Bureau of Narcotics (a precursor to the DEA) was established in July 1930. He held this position through six presidential administrations before finally resigning in 1962.

Anslinger was a total lunatic who built his anti-marijuana stance through scare tactics, racism and deceit. The reason why everyone in America was so afraid of cannabis during the middle of the 20th Century is because Anslinger was lying his ass off.

But you don't have to take my word for it. Read these disturbing quotes straight from the man himself, and you'll discover the real reason why cannabis was originally outlawed in this country.

This evil bigot made up outrageous lies about marijuana, then presented them to Congress and our president as the truth.

Commissioner Henry J. Anslinger's Ridiculous Lies about Marijuana:

- "Marijuana is the most violence-causing drug in the history of mankind."
- "You smoke a joint and you're likely to kill your brother."
- "Marijuana is an addictive drug which produces in its users insanity, criminality, and death."
- "Marijuana leads to pacifism and communist brainwashing."
- "Marijuana use is the certain first step on the road to heroin addiction."
- "How many murders, suicides, robberies, criminal assaults, holdups, burglaries and deeds of maniacal

insanity it causes each year, especially among the young, can only be conjectured."

- "No one knows when he places a marijuana cigarette to his lips, whether he will become a joyous reveler in a musical heaven, a mad insensate, a calm philosopher, or a murderer."

- "It affects different individuals in different ways...Some people will fly into a delirious rage, and they are temporarily irresponsible and may commit violent crimes."

- "Marijuana is a short cut to the insane asylum."

- "Smoke marijuana cigarettes for a month and what was once your brain will be nothing but a storehouse of horrid specters."

Henry J. Anslinger's Racist Quotes about Marijuana Users:

- "The primary reason to outlaw marijuana is its effect on the degenerate races."

- "Reefer makes darkies think they're just as good as a white man."

- "Marijuana makes black men look twice at white women."

- "This marijuana causes white women to seek sexual relations with Negroes, entertainers and any others."

- "There are 100,000 total marijuana smokers in the US, and most are Negroes, Hispanics, Filipinos and entertainers. Their Satanic music, jazz and swing, result from marijuana usage."

It's truly mortifying to consider that this lying, racist scumbag was in charge of America's top drug enforcement organization for over three decades. Anslinger utilized bigotry and fear to frighten the public and convince Congress that marijuana triggers violent killing sprees, while completely ignoring statements from the American Medical Association regarding the potential medical benefits of cannabis.

Anyone who claims that marijuana is "the most violence-causing drug in the history of mankind" has absolutely no credibility. Alcohol consumption will instigate more violence in the United States tonight than marijuana has caused worldwide during the past 10,000 years combined.

If we can all agree that Anslinger was a complete lunatic with zero integrity, it seems logical that we can also reach similar conclusions about the laws he created. Yet here we are 76 years later, and the federal government's stance on marijuana is still firmly rooted in this paranoid 1930s climate of Reefer Madness.

Cannabis is still classified as a Schedule I drug, which is reserved for the most dangerous, addictive drugs that have no medical benefit. In the eyes of the federal government, marijuana is more dangerous and addictive than methamphetamines.

Wait a second.... Uncle Sam actually thinks marijuana is more dangerous and addictive than meth?!? That's the biggest pile of bullshit in the barnyard.

How can anyone take these duplicitous marijuana laws seriously when they defy all truth, logic and common sense?

America's Longtime 'Expert' on Marijuana was Batshit Crazy

"The marijuana user, freed from the restraint of gravitation, bumps his head against the sky. Street lights become orangutans, with eyes of fire. Huge slimy snakes crawl through small cracks in the sidewalk, and prehistoric monsters, intent on his destruction, emerge from keyholes, and pursue him down the street. He feels squirrels walking over his back, while he is being pelted by some unseen enemy with lightning bolts."

- From *On the Trail of Marihuana: The Weed of Madness* (1939) by Earle Albert Rowell & Robert Rowell

What if I told you that America's leading government expert on marijuana testified that he turned into a bat and flew around the room after taking two hits from a joint?

The sensationalist headline "Killer Drug Turns Doctor to Bat!" blared across the front page of the Newark Star-Ledger on October 12, 1938. The headline was attached to a story about a murder trial being held in New York City.

Unscrupulous lawyers during this decade were capitalizing on the ongoing reefer madness and employing a very dishonest defense strategy for clients facing murder charges. Defense attorneys were contending that their clients were innocent because smoking marijuana made them temporarily go insane and kill people.

A highly-publicized murder trial in New York featured testimony from Dr. James C. Munch, a pharmacologist from Temple University. Dr. Munch was called to the stand by a defense attorney and testified under oath that after taking two puffs from a marijuana cigarette, he suddenly morphed into a bat, flew around the room for 15 minutes, and ended up at the bottom of a giant inkwell that was 200 feet deep.

If someone told you they smoked marijuana and turned into a bat, you'd probably say they were batshit crazy. Especially since there's never been a single occurrence in human history where a person has been magically transformed into an animal. Yet this educated, medical professional testified under oath that marijuana did exactly that.

Sounds ridiculous, right?

Hold on. It gets worse. Way worse.

Remember our old buddy Henry J. Anslinger from the last chapter? Well, Commissioner Anslinger thought so highly of Dr. Munch that he appointed him as "Official Expert of the Federal Bureau of Narcotics about Marijuana", a position which Munch held from 1938 to 1962.

Are you fucking kidding me?

Let's get this straight. Henry J. Anslinger and Dr. James Munch were America's foremost authorities on cannabis for the better part of three decades. Anslinger said that marijuana is the most violence-causing drug in the history of mankind, while Munch testified under oath that two puffs from a joint turned him into a bat.

If you ever wanted to know why America's laws against marijuana are so insane, just consider that inmates have been running the asylum since the 1930s.

The United States must legalize marijuana in 2015.

Federal Agencies Have Conflicting Views on Cannabis

"Regardless of where one stands on the broader drug war, we should all be able to agree on the subject of medical marijuana. Here, the use of an otherwise prohibited substance has been found to relieve unbearable suffering in countless patients. How can we fail to support liberty and individual responsibility in such a clear cut case? What harm does it do to anyone else to allow fellow human beings in pain to find the relief they need?"

- **Ron Paul**, Texas Congressman and Presidential Candidate

The Drug Enforcement Agency (**DEA**), the Food and Drug Administration (**FDA**) and the Department of Health and Human Services (**DHHS**) are all headquartered in the Washington D.C. area. They all operate under the umbrella of the United States government. Yet these three agencies have totally contradictory viewpoints on the medical value of marijuana.

The DHHS deals in scientific fact, while the folks at the DEA and FDA conveniently stick with fiction. Some folks might call this a bureaucratic cannabis contradiction. The DEA and the FDA both attack natural herbal medicine while promoting patented pharmaceutical drugs.

The FDA's official position on medical marijuana:

> "No sound scientific studies support medical use of marijuana for treatment in the United States, and no animal or human data support the safety or efficacy of marijuana for general medical use."

For readers who are unaware, the FDA is a lapdog for the multi-billion dollar pharmaceutical industry. Want proof? Look at the case "Zohydro ER", a new opiate-based drug which was released in spring 2014.

This hydrocodone-based painkiller seems like it was specifically engineered for addicts. Unlike other opiate drugs, Zohydro comes in a capsule, which means it can easily be cracked open and snorted. It is five to ten times more powerful than any opiate-based medication currently on the market.

Two years ago, an FDA review panel voted 11-2 against approving Zohydro. Seems like a pretty decisive vote, right? Yet somehow this advisory panel was overruled by their FDA superiors, who said the benefits of Zohydro outweigh the risks.

The medical community is absolutely stunned that this powerful painkiller received FDA approval. Dr. Andrew Kolodny, president of Physicians for Responsible Opioid Prescribing, called the pending release of Zohydro "shocking, outrageous and genuinely frightening." He insists that the powerful painkiller "will kill people as soon as it's released."

The manufacturer warns users on the label that taking Zohydro will expose them to "risks of addiction, abuse, and misuse, which can lead to overdose and death."

Yikes.

Now let's see what the DEA has to say about medical cannabis.

The DEA's official position on medical marijuana:

> "Having no current accepted medical use in the United States and a high potential for abuse, cannabis is a Schedule I controlled substance. The topic of legalizing marijuana for medical use is a controversial issue since the therapeutic properties of marijuana are presently at question when claiming medicinal purpose."

So the DEA insists that cannabis is dangerous, highly addictive and has no medical value. But that claim is totally invalidated by the actions of their governmental counterparts at the DHHS, who currently own U.S. patent 6,630,507 for the medical use of cannabinoids as antioxidants and neuroprotectants.

It's one thing for the FDA and DEA to blatantly ignore the mountains of medical and scientific research on marijuana. It's an entirely different matter, however, when they are ignoring the conclusions reached by the DHHS, one of their sister agencies within the U.S. government.

Congress needs to ask FDA and DEA officials the following question: if marijuana has no medical value, then why does the government own this patent for the medical use of cannabinoids as antioxidants and neuroprotectants?

ABSTRACT OF U.S. PATENT 6,630,507:

"Cannabinoids have been found to have antioxidant properties, unrelated to NMDA receptor antagonism. This new found property makes cannabinoids useful in the treatment and prophylaxis of wide variety of oxidation associated diseases, such as ischemic, age-related, inflammatory and autoimmune diseases. The cannabinoids are found to have particular application as neuroprotectants, for example in limiting neurological damage following ischemic insults, such as stroke and trauma, or in the treatment of neurodegenerative diseases, such as Alzheimer's disease, Parkinson's disease and HIV dementia. Nonpsychoactive cannabinoids, such as cannabidoil, are particularly advantageous to use because they avoid toxicity that is encountered with psychoactive cannabinoids at high doses useful in the method of the present invention."

It would be impossible for this patent to exist unless cannabis had been proven scientifically to have medical benefits.

Absolutely impossible.

This one solitary patent, filed by the U.S. government and funded by the American taxpayer, not only contradicts the shared position of the FDA and DEA that cannabis has no medical value, but it should also nullify the federal government's classification of cannabis as a Schedule I drug.

But despite all scientific evidence to the contrary, cannabis *still* remains classified as a Schedule I drug according to the Controlled Substances Act of 1970. This designation is reserved for the most dangerous drugs that meet the following three criteria.

Criteria for Schedule I controlled substances:

- No currently accepted medical use in the United States
- High potential for abuse
- Lack of accepted safety for use under medical supervision

Classifying marijuana as a Schedule I drug is incredibly offensive to anyone with two eyes, two ears and a brain.

Marijuana is less addictive than coffee, cigarettes or alcohol. In the history of humanity, there has never been a single death attributed to consuming cannabis. Unlike alcohol, heroin or cocaine, it's impossible to die from a marijuana overdose.

Yet the government agency known as the Drug Enforcement Agency (DEA) continues to damage their credibility by insisting that marijuana is more dangerous and addictive than Schedule II drugs like methamphetamine, cocaine and oxycodone.

Ask any police officer if they think cannabis is more dangerous than meth. Ask any drug counselor if they think marijuana is more addictive than Oxycodone. People on the front lines of the drug war will tell you that marijuana doesn't cause violent behavior or lead people to commit crimes to fuel their addictive habit.

When the government tells us that marijuana is more dangerous and addictive than meth, it's impossible to take these classifications seriously. Marijuana should have been downgraded from Schedule I ten years ago when the DHHS was granted U.S. Patent 6,630,507.

Our tax dollars funded the government research that proves cannabis has two undeniable medical benefits. This research then spurred the Department of Health and Human Services to file a patent for two specific medical benefits delivered by *Cannabis sativa*. But instead of circulating a government-wide memo letting everyone know that marijuana has been found to have medical value, each of these agencies operates in a vacuum.

The DEA doesn't care what the DHHS thinks about marijuana. And that's especially true if the DHHS has conducted research that could render their jobs irrelevant. Each year the American taxpayers provide the DEA with $2 billion in funding. And since marijuana is the most popular illegal drug in the United States, you can be certain the DEA won't waver from the hardline position on marijuana anytime soon.

When it comes to having an honest discussion about marijuana, how could anyone believe anything that the DEA says? Science and medicine are being completely disregarded by the organization that stands to suffer most if the news spreads.

If all drugs were legalized today, we could shut the doors on the DEA this afternoon and they would all be looking for new jobs. Imagine if marijuana were legalized today. It would be the same result, just on a smaller scale. And that's exactly what has DEA officials so concerned.

We all need to accept one cold hard truth: it's a poor business decision for the DEA to admit that marijuana has medical value. DEA officials will continue to ignore the truth about marijuana until they retire or die. Human nature dictates that anyone in their shoes would do the same thing.

Any DEA agent who might be brave enough to push for marijuana legalization would be viewed as a pariah within the ranks. His treatment within the agency would be worse than a Coca-Cola executive who admits soda makes you fat, or an accountant who says we should switch to a flat tax system. It might be the right thing to do for the country, but most folks will choose a steady paycheck over truth, justice and the American way.

How can we take anything the DEA says seriously when they are flat-out lying to us about marijuana! Science, medicine and our own personal experience tell us that this all total fucking bullshit.

If marijuana has no medicinal benefits, why are so many terminally ill patients turning to it to improve their quality of life? Why have voters in 23 states approved laws legalizing medical marijuana? It's obvious that the voting public has done more homework on the medical benefits of marijuana than the FDA or DEA.

The self-preservationists at the DEA should take a moment to consider this quote from former President Ronald Reagan: "Government exists to protect us from each other. Where government has gone beyond its limits is in deciding to protect us from ourselves."

Both the FDA and DEA are putting profits ahead of public health. They both support addictive, patented, synthetic medicine. They have even approved marijuana in pill form. But if you plant a seed and grow your own, your ass is getting tossed in the slammer.

Even the DEA's own administrative law judge, Francis Young, says that "marijuana has been accepted as capable of relieving the distress of great numbers of very ill people, and doing so with safety under medical supervision. It would be unreasonable, arbitrary and capricious for DEA to continue to stand between those sufferers and the benefits of this substance in light of the evidence in this record."

This insanity must stop now. The FDA and DEA are lying to us and making things worse. We are legalizing addictive drugs like fucking Zohydro while the world's safest natural pain medicine remains illegal.

Stop putting profits over people!

Legalize cannabis in the United States now and redirect our resources towards getting these deadly opiate drugs off the street!

Marijuana is Legally Grown at Ole Miss by Uncle Sam

"Smoked marijuana has never been, and will never be scientifically approved for medical use."

- From the DEA pamphlet '*Speaking out against Drug Legalization*'

It is impossible for Uncle Sam to tell the American people that marijuana has no medical value when our federal government has been growing it in Mississippi and shipping it to qualified patients for nearly 50 years.

The only federally sanctioned cannabis farm in the United States can be found inside the Coy W. Waller Laboratory Complex on the campus of the University of Mississippi. The good folks down at Ole Miss have been contracted by the National Institute on Drug Abuse to legally grow, harvest and process cannabis.

The Mississippi-grown marijuana is then shipped it to licensed facilities across the country for research purposes. This cannabis growing operation, which is officially known as the Compassionate Investigational New Drug program, also supplies marijuana to a small number of patients who are able to prove it's the only therapeutic drug that can relieve their symptoms.

Federal authorities send a tin canister filled with about 300 pre-rolled marijuana cigarettes to these qualified patients every month. Only 4 patients currently receive cannabis from the U.S. government through this program. Uncle Sam stopped accepting new applications back in 1992, so this program dies when the last remaining patient does.

One of these four patients is 73-year old Elvy Musikka, who suffers from glaucoma and has been enrolled in the program for 30 years. Musikka says she would have lost her sight several years ago if it wasn't for medical cannabis.

"In 1975, my doctor told me if I didn't start using marijuana, I'd go blind. Shortly thereafter I found out that, indeed, it was the only thing that would help me with my glaucoma," said Musikka.

"All of us admitted in the program were required to prove to the FDA, DEA and NIDA that marijuana was the safest and most efficient treatment available for us. The bottom line for me was that I was losing my sight."

Stop. Hold up a second. Rewind that back.

Did you hear what Elvy Musikka just said?

31

She said that all patients are required to convince both the FDA and the DEA that cannabis is the safest medicine for their illness.

But I thought the official position of these two agencies is that cannabis has no accepted medical value in the United States!? What the hell is going on here?

How can the FDA and DEA possibly approve applications for patients to use marijuana as medicine, or even create the application form itself, if it has no accepted medical value?

The federal government says the marijuana isn't medicine, but how can we believe that bullshit when Uncle Sam himself has been growing and shipping medical cannabis across the country for the past 50 years?

"There is no state, no place, where people do not seriously need this medicine. There is public support for all of us, everywhere. We have five generations of lies and misinformation keeping us incapable of rendering rational decisions as individuals, or as a nation, on this issue"

The man who oversees the federally funded Marijuana Project at Ole Miss is a man named Mahmoud El-Sohly. He says that since smoking is not a pharmaceutically acceptable form of delivery, he's been working on alternative ways to deliver the drug. His first idea for a delivery device was a suppository. As you might imagine, this idea didn't thrill many patients.

"People really don't like suppositories, so it really didn't make it on the market."

Gee, I wonder why?

Isn't he basically just telling all marijuana users who prefer to smoke, eat or vaporize cannabis that they can shove it up their ass? Even though this was an atrocious idea by Mahmoud El-Sohly, I owe him a huge debt of gratitude for providing the perfect analogy for Uncle Sam's war on drugs.

All Americans want to do is enjoy this wonderful plant in peace, in any way they see fit, without fear of being persecuted. Meanwhile, Uncle Sam wants to turn weed into a pill that we can all shove up our asses.

This is asinine. The United States must legalize cannabis in 2015.

The Anti-Marijuana Faction is Driven by Fear and Hate

"If I do not believe as you believe, it proves that you do not believe as I believe, and that is all that it proves."

- **Thomas Paine**, *Common Sense* (1776)

The people who are most vehemently opposed to marijuana legalization in America usually have one thing in common. They've never tried it before. Their sanctimonious protests against this magnificent plant are rooted in ignorance, fear and hatred.

Let's examine two separate interviews from last year involving CNN Headline News anchor Nancy Grace and conservative political pundit Ann Coulter. Even though these interviews transpired just last year, they feature remarks that appear to be straight from the 1930s.

During a January 2014 interview with Mason Tvert of the Marijuana Policy Project, anchor Nancy Grace made the outrageous allegation that marijuana causes people to "shoot each other, stab each other, strangle each other, drive under the influence, kill families… wipe out a whole family!"

You've gotta be fucking kidding me. Nancy Grace obviously has very checkered history when it comes to courting controversy. Just google the stories about her fiancé's murder, the suicide of interviewee Melinda Duckett and her coverage of the Caylee Anthony case).

But claiming that marijuana will turn you into a violent killer who stabs, shoots and strangles entire families? These are outrageous, boldfaced, bullshit lies. No television network with an ounce of journalistic integrity should allow this idiotic woman to open her mouth. But then again, we are talking about CNN here. Their last remaining shred of editorial dignity flew out the window when their coverage of missing Malaysia Airlines Flight 370 entered its fifth month of speculation on whether aliens, an asteroid or Bane from Batman could have taken down the aircraft.

Ask any emergency room doctor or police officer if marijuana makes people violent. They'll tell you that Nancy Grace is a lying cretin who needs to have her media credentials revoked immediately. Marijuana use has never been linked to violence by anyone fights crime on the front lines. In fact, the opposite holds true. Marijuana use is inversely related to violent behavior. This wondrous herb is highly renowned in many religions and cultures for its ability to bring people together and allow them to bond on a deeper level.

Now let's fast-forward one week later to the CNN talk show *Piers Morgan Live*, where Morgan's guest was conservative political commentator Ann Coulter. During an exchange about the potential benefits of cannabis, Coulter unleashed a rambling diatribe that had reasonable viewers raising two middle fingers at their television screens.

"If it is made legal, vastly more people will take it and it will be a disaster for commerce, because potheads are incapable of following simple instructions and getting a job done," said Coulter. "You can't get anything done with a pothead... I'm going to be paying for their food, housing and now for their health care apparently, because they can't perform any useful jobs."

When Piers Morgan asked her to clarify her statement, Coulter instead shared this anecdote about a guy who was supposed to clean her swimming pool a few years ago.

"When I moved to a new place in California and there was a pool, and the pool guy didn't, you know... I come back then it's four feet down, it's covered with green mold. And I called him up, he was a pothead. So I took three pictures and henceforth that was my argument."

Everyone got that? One solitary incident involving her pool cleaning guy a few years ago has provided Ann Coulter with all the statistical data she needs to deliver a mass pronouncement on the overall work ethic of weed smokers. This tired old stereotype is frequently used by alcohol drinkers like Coulter, who claim to be experts on marijuana despite having never tried it.

Cannabis smokers aren't lazy. Millions of hard-working, successful professionals across the USA got high today. Titans of business and industry who have built some of the most powerful companies on earth have publicly confirmed that they've smoked marijuana. Has anyone ever called Steve Jobs, Bill Gates, Ted Turner or Michael Bloomberg a lazy pothead?

Brilliant scientists such as Nobel Prize winners Kary Mullis (chemistry) and Richard Feynman (physics), astronomer Carl Sagan and biologist Stephen Jay Gould have all endorsed the use of cannabis to expand their thinking and view subject matter in a new light. Francis Crick, who won the 1962 Nobel Prize in Physiology for discovering the double-helix structure of DNA, was a founding member of the cannabis legalization group Soma.

Barack Obama and Bill Clinton both smoked weed when they were younger and both became President of the United States. Coincidence? Nope.

The most prolific artists, entertainers and musicians of our time have smoked the noble herb. That list alone could fill an entire book, and includes a few names which might be familiar to some readers, including The Beatles, Madonna, Oprah Winfrey, David Letterman and Martha Stewart. If the Rock n'

Roll Hall of Fame had a policy against electing musicians who used marijuana, the entire building would be empty.

Despite all evidence to the contrary, Ann Coulter contends that legalizing marijuana will lead to total economic collapse, all because Bill Murray from *Caddyshack* took a giant dump in her pool and drained it halfway after discovering that his client was demon spawn from the seventh circle of hell.

Imagine presenting Coulter with this scenario. Last week her neighbor left the local bar and got behind the wheel after drinking 5 beers in two hours. On the way home, he accidentally ran through a stop sign, slammed into another car and killed the other driver.

Using Coulter's skewed logic, this one incident provides us with plenty of statistical data. We can now conclude that anyone who drinks alcohol is a murderer. Therefore, no one should ever be allowed to drink again.

Grace and Coulter are quite certain that marijuana will turn you into an unemployed murderer who stabs people and poops in their pool. But their alarmist anti-marijuana positions have no basis in reality. They've been told all their lives that marijuana was bad, so it must be true.

Instead of approaching the topic with an inquisitive mind and an open heart, like Dr. Sanjay Gupta and Dr. Lester Grinspoon, these two women have chosen to ignore the mountains scientific evidence and thousands of testimonials that vouch for the goodness of cannabis.

Their ignorant viewpoints on cannabis remind me of the Dr. Seuss book *Green Eggs and Ham*. They would not like marijuana here or there. They would not like it anywhere.

But if they would just let their guard down and give it a try, it might bring a smile to their face and a twinkle to their eye. "Hey, I like this green plant! Well, I'll be damned! Thank you, thank you, Cannabis man."

It never fails. The people most fervidly opposed to marijuana legalization in the United States are exactly the type of closed-minded individuals who would stand to benefit the most from the mind-expanding properties of cannabis.

CHAPTER 2: THE PUNISHMENT DOES NOT FIT THE CRIME

"Penalties against possession of a drug should not be more damaging to an individual than the use of the drug itself; and where they are, they should be changed. Nowhere is this more clear than in the laws against possession of marijuana in private for personal use."

- Former U.S. President **Jimmy Carter**

When President Richard Nixon announced in 1971 that the United States government was launching a "war on drugs", no one could have imagined it would be the longest, costliest conflict in our nation's history.

During the 1980s, President Ronald Reagan continued Nixon's initiative by making the war on drugs a core component of his political platform. Throughout the decade, many state governments followed the president's lead by passing stricter laws and punishments for marijuana-related crimes. This predictably led to a surge in the number of Americans getting arrested. Many of these harsh laws from the Eighties are still on the books today.

Between 1996 and 2012, police arrested over 11.4 million Americans for possession of marijuana. More people get arrested for marijuana in America each year than all other drugs combined. There were roughly 1.5 million drug-related arrests made by police in 2011, and over half of those arrests were for marijuana.

Thousands of our fellow citizens get arrested every day for the benign act of being caught with cannabis. According to the FBI Uniform Crimes Report, roughly 88% of all marijuana arrests in the United States are for simple possession.

Small-time marijuana farmers receive harsher jail sentences than murderers and rapists in several U.S. states. Even if you don't spend time in jail, having a drug arrest on your record can permanently damage your chances of qualifying for student loans or getting a decent job.

There is a huge disparity in how marijuana-related offenses are handled across the 50 states. Just consider that in the state of Wyoming (which shares a border with Colorado), a person who gets caught with just a teeny-weeny, microscopic baby nugget in their front pocket can still get handed a whopping one year jail sentence and $1,000 fine.

Here are some examples of the harsh, oppressive laws against marijuana users in America.

US States with Oppressive Laws against Cannabis:

- **KANSAS**: If you are caught cultivating five marijuana plants, you will face a prison sentence of 12 to 17 years.

- **WYOMING**: A person found under the influence of marijuana in public will be charged with a misdemeanor, which is punishable by 90 days in jail and a $100 fine.

- **LOUISIANA**: Distribution or cultivation of any amount of marijuana requires a mandatory five year jail sentence.

- **VIRGINIA**: Cultivation of any amount of marijuana is considered a felony which is punishable by five to 30 years in prison, along with a hefty $10,000 fine.

- **IDAHO**: A person found under the influence of marijuana in public will be charged with a misdemeanor, which is punishable by six months in jail and a $1,000 fine.

Anyone notice a trend here? States on the west coast have more liberal voters and are more likely to have legalized cannabis for medical or recreational reasons, while states throughout the South and the Midwest have much stricter anti-marijuana laws with considerably harsher punishments.

The marijuana laws across the 50 states are fundamentally different. To truly understand the absurdity of the situation, just compare Colorado to any of its neighbors. Adults in Colorado can legally grow up to six marijuana plants and purchase cannabis recreationally from hundreds of stores across the state.

Colorado happens to share a 50 mile long state border with Oklahoma. If you are unlucky enough to get caught twice with a small nugget of weed in the Sooner State, you will face felony charges and spend up to ten years in prison.

Therefore, anyone in Oklahoma who insists on using marijuana has only two options:

1. Break the law
2. Move to a marijuana-friendly state

It's ludicrous that your sister in Colorado can conveniently purchase cannabis anytime from her friendly neighborhood dispensary, but your brother in Oklahoma won't be getting out of prison until 2024 because the cops found a roach in his car's ashtray.

Arresting people for marijuana-related offenses extracts an enormous human toll. Punishing people with a few years in prison is bad enough, but charging anyone with a felony is effectively giving that person a lifetime sentence. Having a felony on your record means you can't apply for certain jobs, you can't receive student loans and you lose your right to vote.

Punishing patients for seeking pain relief is barbaric, unjust and inhumane. The real crime here is forcing sick people to decide whether they should move to a state with liberal marijuana laws or stay put and risk being arrested. This ethical and moral dilemma must be heavily weighed and publically debated by President Obama and Congress.

How much longer can this madness continue?

The United States must legalize marijuana in 2015.

Arresting Patients for Seeking Pain Relief is Barbaric

"It is beyond my comprehension that any humane person would withhold such a beneficial substance from people in such great need, simply because others use it for different purposes."

- Paleontologist **Stephen Jay Gould**

The U.S. federal government refuses to consider the mountains of scientific research and thousands of glowing, firsthand testimonials from medical cannabis patients. We are disregarding basic standards of human decency in favor of arresting any citizen who decides to use marijuana to relieve their symptoms.

Arresting sick people for the crime of acquiring medicine that will help them feel better is a barbaric act. A cancer patient in Kansas who knows cannabis is the only medicine that will reduce their nausea is faced with three bleak choices: break the law and risk arrest, move to a different state or suffer in agony. For any society that values freedom, this is a disgraceful situation.

Marijuana might be the only medicine providing effective relief for Aunt Betsy's glaucoma in Tennessee. Cannabis could be helping her live a happier and healthier life. But if Aunt Betsy had the audacity to grow her own cannabis in the backyard to save money on her limited income, she could get locked away in a cage for several years, regardless of what her doctors tell the judge.

Folks, before we go any further, you've gotta understand this simple fact: cannabis is a pain reliever that comes in seed form. Just plant the seed, add sunshine and water, and two months later you've got a big fat jar of free homegrown medicine.

But when you grow your own medicine, no one makes money. That's why Uncle Sam and the lobbyists for Big Pharma have been so stubborn about keeping cannabis illegal. The only medicine that is copasetic with Uncle Sam is the synthetic stuff made by publically traded companies.

Just put yourself in Aunt Betsy's shoes. Thousands of glaucoma patients have already posted testimonials about the effectiveness of marijuana on their condition. Since Aunt Betsy is terrified that she might lose her sight in the next couple years, she decides to experiment with cannabis. And she discovers the plant is a godsend.

Now what should Aunt Betsy do? Moving to a state like Colorado or Washington is completely out of the question, since she is on limited income and all of her immediate family lives in Tennessee. And since the cost of purchasing the plant on the black market is so exorbitant, she couldn't possibly afford the steady supply she would need to prevent blindness.

Desperate for relief and facing almost certain blindness, Aunt Betsy decides to discretely grow a few cannabis plants in her backyard. In Tennessee, a person caught growing just one cannabis plant can be charged with a felony and spend six years in jail.

Imagine your aunt, grandmother, sister or mom being locked behind bars for growing a medicinal plant in her backyard. But it's been that way across the USA for 76 years and counting.

Punishing patients for seeking relief from their symptoms is barbaric way for a government to treat their sick citizens. If someone suffering from cancer says that marijuana stimulates their appetite and allows them to consume a nourishing meal, common sense dictates that it would be criminal to prevent this person from using medicine.

The United States must legalize marijuana in 2015.

Release All Citizens in Jail for Marijuana Possession

"It's just the stupidest law possible... You're just making criminals out of people who aren't engaged in criminal activity. And we're spending zillions of dollars trying to fight a war we can't win! We could make zillions, just legalize it and tax it like we do liquor."

- Academy Award-winning Actor **Morgan Freeman**

The United States needs to immediately release all citizens who are currently imprisoned for nonviolent cannabis-related crimes.

If America granted immediate amnesty to all the prisoners currently serving time for cannabis-related offenses and expunged their crimes, it would immediately free up 50,000 cells in our overcrowded jails and prisons. It would save taxpayers about $1 billion each year. Most importantly, the people who have suffered unfairly under our nation's oppressive cannabis laws could re-enter society without the stigma of having a prior drug arrest on their record.

Consider the case of Colorado, where tens of thousands of people have been arrested for simple cannabis possession over the past couple decades. According to the FBI, there were 210,000 marijuana-possession arrests in Colorado over the past 25 years. More than 25,000 people were arrested for cannabis possession in Colorado just between 2006 and 2010.

Some folks assume that anyone serving time for marijuana possession in Colorado would be automatically released on January 1st, 2014. Now that it's legal for adults to buy cannabis in dozens of licensed dispensaries, why should the guy who got caught with cannabis back in 2012 still be in the slammer?

If the USA had laws similar the rest of the free world, anyone currently in jail for marijuana possession would immediately be released and have their sentences commuted right after marijuana legalization went into effect. This is called retroactive ameliorative relief, and America is totally in the Stone Ages when it comes to guaranteeing this right.

There are only 22 countries in the world that don't guarantee retroactive ameliorative relief in sentencing. Nations like Pakistan, South Sudan, Myanmar and…the United States.

By legalizing cannabis and introducing retroactive ameliorative relief into our legal system, we could positively alter the lives of 50,000 Americans and save $1 billion annually.

The United States must legalize marijuana in 2015.

CHAPTER 3: INDUSTRIES AGAINST LEGALIZATION

Question: What do police officers and drug cartels have in common with alcohol, tobacco and pharmaceutical drug companies?

Answer: They are all fiercely opposed to the legalization of marijuana because of the negative impact it will have on their livelihoods.

Follow the money and it's plain to see why the alcohol, pharmaceutical, and tobacco industries are united in their opposition to marijuana legalization.

Not only is cannabis less addictive, less toxic and more effective than any product they currently produce, but you can grow it at home quite easily. Nobody makes money off that.

- ✓ Pharmaceutical drugs kill **100,000** Americans each year
- ✓ Alcohol abuse kills **75,000** Americans each year
- ✓ Marijuana has never killed anyone. It is physically impossible to overdose.

Big Pharma

"One to two thousand people in the U.S. die every year from Aspirin. But no one has ever documented a death from marijuana."

- **Dr. Lester Grinspoon**, Professor of Psychiatry at Harvard Medical School

Many highly-regarded economic analysts agree that pharmaceutical firms would experience a huge loss of revenue if cannabis were legalized.

Pharmaceutical drug manufacturers are projected to generate over $1 trillion in global revenue this year through the development and distribution of synthetically manufactured, highly addictive and heavily advertised prescription pills.

The first priority for these companies isn't improving the overall health of the world's population. These are publicly traded companies with demanding shareholders who value profits over people. The number one objective for any drug company CEO is to make Wall Street happy.

Billion dollar advertising campaigns and loose prescription writing from shady pain clinics and physicians are two huge reasons why Big Pharma has been raking in big profits throughout the 2000s. The quarterly earnings reports might make Wall Street smile, but these profits have come at a tremendous cost.

Soaring revenues generated by the pharmaceutical industry throughout the 2000s have been mirrored by an escalating prescription drug epidemic that has wreaked havoc on families and communities across America.

People are initially getting hooked on expensive, opiate-based painkillers like Percocet, Vicodin and Oxycodone. Depending on the dosage involved, these pills can cost anywhere from $20 to $75 on the street. This adds up to quite an expensive habit when your addiction is driving you to buy pills every day.

People who are addicted to opiate-based painkillers have only one mission in life, and that's to find their next fix. And if their daily quest to score pills is unsuccessful, they will be facing horrible withdrawal symptoms. Since prescription drugs are so expensive on the street, broke addicts who are desperate to stave off withdrawal are switching to a more affordable alternative: heroin.

Heroin and most prescription painkillers are sourced from the same opium poppy plant, *Papaver somniferum*. Since a packet of heroin only costs $10 in an east coast city like Philadelphia, opiate addicts are now switching from pills to heroin in droves. Heroin is simply a much cheaper way to get opiates into their bloodstream.

America is now facing a full-blown heroin addiction crisis, which was essentially reverse engineered by the pharmaceutical industry. Nearly 80% of recent heroin users got hooked on prescription painkillers first, according to a 2013 study from the Center for Behavioral Health Statistics and Quality.

Drug overdose is now the leading cause of injury death in the United States. Each day an average of 105 people die from drug overdoses in the USA, a number which has tripled since 1990. Painkiller pills are responsible for almost 75% of prescription drug overdoses according to the Centers for Disease Control and Prevention. Nearly 60 percent of all drug overdose deaths (22,134) involved pharmaceutical drugs in 2010, more than heroin and cocaine combined.

Best-selling anti-depressant drugs like Zoloft and Prozac can cause a slew of scary side effects, including hypertension, hair loss, nausea, diarrhea and seizures. But the black box warning which is now mandatory on all anti-depressant packaging is the most frightening of all. It reads: "antidepressants may increase the risk of suicide in people younger than 25."

Can someone please explain why are we giving depressed people Zoloft and Prozac instead of cannabis to fight their illness, when the side effects of these pills are more damaging than the actual condition they are trying to treat?

The anti-depressant drug Cannabis has few side effects. No one has ever had a seizure after smoking it. In fact, many people use cannabis to control their seizures. It relaxes your muscles, eases your mind and lowers your blood pressure.

Dr. Lester Grinspoon, professor of psychiatry emeritus at Harvard Medical School and author of the book *Marijuana Reconsidered*, explains that the pharmaceutical companies already recognize that "marijuana is so versatile in treating everything from Crohn's disease to nausea to premenstrual syndrome that once it can be produced in an economy of scale and free of prohibition tariffs it would sweep all these artificially expensive pharmaceutical products on the market aside."

Let's recap, shall we?

Pharmaceutical drugs are now the leading cause of injury death in this country, yet they are totally legal to purchase with a prescription. Cannabis is a natural plant which has never caused an overdose death and is not physically addictive. But here in America, patients are getting arrested and thrown in jail for opting to use the safer, natural medicine.

This is sheer lunacy. We must stop putting profits over people and legalize marijuana in the United States in 2015.

Big Alcohol

"Herb is the healing of a nation. Alcohol is the destruction."

- Reggae music legend **Bob Marley**

One of the main arguments against legalizing cannabis is that it's deemed a "gateway drug" which will lead to further experimentation with more dangerous substances down the road.

But if cannabis is considered to be a gateway drug, then someone needs to explain where alcohol fits into this equation. For most American adults, alcohol was their first introduction to a mind-altering substance, not cannabis.

Alcohol is legally sold on every street corner in the country and can be found in the majority of U.S. households. It's served at almost every social and business event in the United States. We are constantly bombarded with advertisements for beer, wine and liquors that show sexy people having fun in exotic locales.

When folks want to relax, celebrate or cope with life's problems, they often pour themselves a drink. Or two. Well, maybe one more can't hurt…

Sometimes folks overdo it and start making foolish decisions they would never consider when sober. Quickly it can spiral out of control with an assault, DUI, car crash or even death.

Since the dawn of humanity, people have consumed substances to alter their consciousness. But if alcohol was introduced tomorrow as a brand new intoxicant, it would quickly be outlawed.

The nonprofit organization Law Enforcement Against Prohibition (LEAP), which is comprised of police officers in favor of marijuana legalization, contends that "If alcohol was a new drug, a national alcohol crisis would be declared."

Alcohol is indisputably the biggest drug problem in the United States, responsible for more injuries, death and destruction than all other illegal drugs combined. The toll it takes on American society every day is shocking, yet it still maintains a ubiquitous presence in our society. We continue to glamorize and advertise alcoholic beverages as if there are no negative consequences, which is a sure-fire way to guarantee our future generations will be riddled with the same societal problems we face today: violent behavior, drunk driving, chronic alcoholism and premature death.

People die from alcohol abuse and drunk drivers every day in all 50 states, but the public would rather avoid this touchy topic and look the other way. Rarely do you see a public service announcement showing the painful consequences of alcohol abuse.

We need to stop burying our heads in the sand and confront this inconvenient truth: your ability to make rational decisions gets weaker with each alcoholic beverage you consume, which is exactly why millions of Americans make the terrible mistake of getting behind the wheel after they've had too much to drink, despite the harsh legal consequences.

Drunk driving continues to be a horrible crisis with an enormous death toll. The damage caused by drunk drivers in America is shocking.

DRUNK DRIVERS ARE A MENACE TO SOCIETY:

- The FBI estimates that 1.2 million DWI arrests took place in 2011.

- Each hour, drunk drivers kill one American and injure 20 Americans.

- One-third of all highway fatalities involve a drunk driver

- Drunk drivers are responsible for nearly 10,000 deaths and 173,000 injuries each year

- According to the National Traffic and Safety Board, the annual cost of impaired driving is a stunning $130 billion.

Alcohol is the primary catalyst in the majority of assaults and violent crimes, while cannabis has the complete opposite effect. It is inversely associated with aggressive behavior.

The list goes on and on... alcohol kills brain cells and makes you fat. Alcohol causes a ton of regret and remorse from people who mimic the *Strange Case of Dr. Jekyll and Mr. Hyde* after a few ounces of alcohol start coursing through their bloodstream. Cancers of the mouth, pharynx, and larynx are all associated with heavy drinking. Alcohol dehydrates your body and causes horrible hangovers.

Dozens of teenagers and young adults die each day due to alcohol poisoning. Thousands more get sent to the hospital to have their stomachs pumped. But it's impossible to ingest a fatal overdose of marijuana.

Everyone should visit the website Sincethismorning.com, which has a running tally of daily deaths directly caused by alcohol versus marijuana. The alcohol deaths number in the thousands. The marijuana column always remains at zero.

We need to stop lying to our children and quit brainwashing our citizens into thinking that alcohol is all fun and games instead of fights and funerals. Cannabis consumption has been endorsed by millions of our fellow citizens, from George Washington and Thomas Jefferson to Woody Harrelson and Snoop Dogg.

Let's present the honest facts on alcohol versus marijuana and give people the freedom to decide for themselves.

Big Tobacco

"Amazingly, smoking is even worse than we knew. Even after 50 years, we're still finding new ways that smoking maims and kills people."

- **Thomas Frieden**, Director of the Centers for Disease Control and Prevention

Cigarettes, if they were introduced today, would be like the 'Riddle of the Sphinx' for Harvard Business School students. "Okay class. Here's the scenario. You have to market a new product. However, there is one giant proviso. It's the only product in the world that when used as intended will kill you."

Mountains of scientific evidence have identified tobacco smoke as the major catalyst in a number of deadly cancers. Marijuana doesn't cause cancer. It kicks cancer in the ass.

According to the National Cancer Institute, cannabis has been shown to kill cancer cells in the laboratory. Cannabis can relieve pain, vomiting and anxiety, which is huge for anyone fighting cancer or recovering from chemotherapy.

Tobacco causes cancer. Marijuana kills cancer cells.

Any questions on which plant should be legal?

Smokers find it notoriously difficult to quit using tobacco, which is why smoking cessation products generated over $2.5 billion in sales last year.

Tobacco users are so desperate to quit their deadly habit that they will try anything (gum, patches, lozenges, inhalers, pills) to help them fight their cravings.

Cannabis must scare the hell out of the tobacco industry. I can't imagine a more perfect replacement for cigarette smokers trying to kick the habit. It can relax your mind, calm your nerves and soothe your tensions. It's not physically addictive and you don't need to smoke hundreds of puffs each day.

The United States must legalize marijuana in 2015.

Police, Prosecutors and the Prison-Industrial Complex

"When a private enterprise fails, it is closed down; when a government enterprise fails, it is expanded. Isn't that exactly what's been happening with drugs?"

- Nobel Prize-winning economist **Milton Friedman**

Take a nationwide survey of all Americans who are currently employed in law enforcement, corrections or at government agencies, and you'll find that 99 percent of them are totally against legalizing cannabis.

The U.S. government spends billions every two weeks just cutting paychecks for the millions of criminal justice professionals tasked with responsibility for arresting, prosecuting and incarcerating their fellow citizens for marijuana possession.

America's ancient federal laws should be considered entrapment. We've created an imbroglio where one out of every three U.S. citizens will be considered federal lawbreakers at some point during their lifetimes. If the status quo continues and marijuana remains illegal under federal law, police will continue to make arrests from this revolving group of 100 million American marijuana users.

Police officers have arrest quotas to meet and mouths to feed. If you're a rookie cop and running dead last on the force in monthly arrests, what's your plan on the final day of May? Should you attempt to infiltrate the dangerous gang that's dealing deadly heroin? Follow a few leads on that unsolved homicide case? Or drive to a local movie theatre showing the new *Harold and Kumar* movie and look for wisps of smoke rising from cracked vehicle windows to pad your arrest record?

The Drug Enforcement Administration (DEA) was created on July 1, 1973, through an executive order issued by President Richard Nixon. The president's goal was to establish a single, unified agency for America to fight "an all-out global war on the drug menace."

When the DEA was originally established forty years ago, it was operating with a $75 million budget and 1,470 special agents. Today it has an annual budget of $2 billion and employs over 5,000 special agents.

No one at the DEA will ever publically admit that marijuana is harmless compared to other drugs like heroin, cocaine and methamphetamines. That would be like the president of Pepsi holding a press conference to announce that soda gives you diabetes. Right now a huge chunk of the DEA's annual budget is dedicated to enforcing our nation's marijuana laws. If

America no longer has any marijuana laws to enforce, guess what happens to that budget?

Here's a hint: name the guy who wore a black top hat and played lead guitar for Guns N' Roses.

James L. Capra, the chief of operations at the DEA, said that the recent legalization of marijuana in Colorado and Washington was "reckless and irresponsible," during a Senate hearing in January 2014. "It scares us. Every part of the world where this has been tried, it has failed time and time again."

Notice how Capra fails to name-drop any nations where legalized cannabis has resulted in negative consequences? That's because he's lying through his teeth. It's impossible for him to back up this vague assertion with concrete data.

Lying to Congress during an official Senate hearing should get your ass fired from the DEA and thrown in jail. But Capra not only lied to Congress, he told them the exact opposite of the truth! In the European nations of Holland and Portugal, the decriminalization of cannabis has actually led to a decrease in marijuana use.

During the same Senate hearing, Capra insisted that legalizing cannabis in Colorado and Washington "is a bad experiment. It's going to cost us in terms of social costs."

I wonder how Capra feels about the societal damage caused by shitfaced people swerving down the street in a speeding two ton metal rectangle. If the acronym "DEA" stood for "Drinking Eradication Agency" instead of "Drug Enforcement Agency", there's no doubt the focus of Capra and his cronies would magically shift overnight. Hopefully, members of Congress will book a future hearing with Capra to discuss how much damage our oppressive marijuana laws have done to millions of nonviolent Americans and their families.

Capra and his DEA colleagues are biased against marijuana for selfish reasons. They aren't really concerned about the social costs of legalization. Deep inside, they are scared shitless about losing their cushy DEA jobs where they get to travel to exotic locales, spy on bad guys, pocket free contraband and pretend they're Crockett and Tubbs.

When Capra tells Congress that legalization is a bad experiment, he's not thinking in terms of social costs. He's thinking about how difficult it will be to make monthly mortgage payments without a weekly paycheck. Legalizing marijuana would render many DEA jobs meaningless; thousands of Capra's colleagues would get their walking papers and the agency would shrink substantially. Police officers, prosecutors, prisons and bail bondsmen would also experience a huge drop in "business" if America ended cannabis prohibition.

Capra and his cronies are utilizing the famous *Chicken Little* technique by telling us that "The sky is falling!" when in reality *The Emperor Wears No Clothes.*

Partnership for a Drug-Free America

The Partnership for a Drug-Free America is a non-profit organization which has received millions of dollars in funding from tobacco, alcohol and pharmaceutical companies since it was founded in 1985.

To the general public, this organization is best known for producing anti-drug public service announcements, including the infamous 1987 television commercial "This is your brain on drugs" with an egg in a frying pan.

The Partnership for a Drug-Free America was heavily criticized after *Village Voice* reporter Cynthia Cotts analyzed years of corporate tax returns and found that the biggest donors were cigarette, alcohol and drug manufacturers. After serious backlash, the organization finally decided to stop receiving funds from alcohol and tobacco companies in 1997. However, they still accept hefty donations from pharmaceutical firms with open arms.

Big Pharma, Big Alcohol and Big Tobacco have donated millions of tax-deductible dollars to the Partnership for a Drug-Free America over the past 30 years. This list of corporate donors clearly shows which companies will stand to lose the most if cannabis were legalized.

Major Corporate Donors to

'Partnership for a Drug-Free America':

- American Brands (later named Fortune Brands, producer of Jim Beam whiskey)
- Anheuser Busch (Budweiser, Michelob, Busch)
- Bristol Meyers-Squibb
- GlaxoSmithKline
- Hoffmann-La Roche
- Merck & Company
- Pfizer
- Philip Morris (Marlboro cigarettes, Miller beer)
- Proctor & Gamble
- R.J. Reynolds (Camel, Salem & Winston cigarettes)

These multi-billion dollar industries are more interested in protecting profits than promoting public health. Marijuana is less harmful, less expensive and more effective than the products they produce. Big Pharma, Big Tobacco and Big Alcohol are rightfully afraid of superior new competition stealing away their longtime customers.

CHAPTER 4: THE TIMES THEY ARE A-CHANGIN'

"I really believe we should treat marijuana the way we treat the beverage alcohol. I've never used marijuana and I don't intend to, but it's just one of those things that I think: this war on drugs just hasn't succeeded."

- **Pat Robertson**, Chairman of the Christian Broadcasting Network (2012)

The American public is finally starting to recognize the absurdity of locking people away for using cannabis. Over the past few years we have witnessed a dramatic shift in public opinion that seems to be accelerating every week.

When Gallup first surveyed the American public for their opinions on marijuana legalization in 1969, only 12% said they were in favor of the move.

But last year, for the first time in history, a majority of Americans (58%) responded "Yes" to the question, "Do you think the use of marijuana should be made legal, or not?" That same Gallup Poll, which was conducted in October 2013, revealed that 38% of Americans have tried cannabis at least once.

The campaign to legalize marijuana in the United States scored two unprecedented victories on November 6, 2012, when enlightened voters in Colorado and Washington both voted in favor of ballot initiatives allowing for the regulation, taxation and consumption of recreational cannabis.

Colorado Amendment 64 was approved by 55% of voters and enacted as Article 18, section 16 of the state constitution. The law officially legalized the "personal use and regulation of marijuana" for adults 21 and over.

After the ballot measure was passed, a special task force was appointed by Governor John Hickenlooper to create new regulations on how marijuana would be grown, sold and taxed. The task force took several months to develop the system and procedures that would regulate cannabis commerce in Colorado. The state now oversees all aspects of the budding industry including retail stores, cultivators, testing facilities and product manufacturers.

The world's first legal recreational marijuana sales took place in Colorado on January 1, 2014 when 37 retail stores across the Centennial State opened for business, garnering global media coverage. The state is now experiencing a tourism boom from out-of-state cannabis aficionados who are visiting specifically to enjoy Colorado's new found status as the Amsterdam of America.

By all accounts, legalization in Colorado is off to a roaring economic success. State officials originally estimated they would collect about $70 million in tax revenue from the cannabis industry in 2014. However, an updated report released from Moody's Investors Service indicates that Colorado will generate nearly $100 million in tax revenue from the marijuana industry this year, a striking 40% increase from original projections.

"We anticipate near-term growth in these revenues as the Colorado market matures and as legalization lessens the appeal of black market sales, which should redistribute revenue from illegal traffickers to state coffers," says Moody's analyst Andrea Unsworth in the report *Colorado's Legalized Marijuana Tax Revenues Exceed Expectations,* which was released on April 11, 2014.

Analysts from Moody's also predict that decriminalization in Colorado will substantially reduce policing costs previously associated with marijuana-related arrests, prosecution, sentencing, and incarceration. This area is tougher to quantify, but it undoubtedly equals millions in additional annual savings for the state.

Colorado now imposes sales and excise taxes on every cannabis-related transaction. There's a 10% sales tax added to all retail purchases, and a 15% excise tax imposed on all wholesale marijuana sales. The state keeps 85% of the additional tax revenue and distributes the remaining 15% to local governments.

Each year henceforth, the first $40 million in tax revenue collected from the cannabis industry is earmarked for Colorado's public school capital construction assistance fund. An additional $10.4 million is allocated for regulatory oversight of the industry and $2 million will be allotted for substance abuse treatment.

Just in Pueblo County alone, local officials estimate that a whopping $1 million in "found revenue" will be added to their county budget this year, with every cent coming from taxes collected off legal cannabis transactions in their county. Right now there are six retail stores operating in Pueblo County, and another four are currently plowing through the rigorous application process.

"Like most local governments for the past four or five years, we've been dealing with a very difficult budget crisis," says Pueblo County commissioner Cal Pace. "This is the first new infusion of revenue for our county in a while of a significant amount."

Next let's examine the situation in Washington, the Evergreen State. More than 56% of Washington voters approved the groundbreaking 2012 ballot measure Initiative 502, which licenses and regulates the production, distribution, and possession of marijuana for adults over 21.

Brief summary of Washington Initiative 502:

"This measure removes state-law prohibitions against producing, processing, and selling marijuana, subject to licensing and regulation by the liquor control board; allow limited possession of marijuana by persons aged twenty-one and over; and impose 25% excise taxes on wholesale and retail sales of marijuana, earmarking revenue for purposes that include substance-abuse prevention, research, education, and healthcare."

Rather than create an entirely new system from scratch like their counterparts in the Rockies, officials in Washington designated their State Liquor Control Board to be the agency responsible for controlling the now-legal industry.

Washington conducted a lottery for marijuana retail licenses from April 21 to 25 and announced the winners of retailer, producer and processor licenses on May 2, 2014. The first legal recreational marijuana stores in Washington are expected to be open by June 2014.

There will be exactly 334 retail dispensaries located throughout Washington. Their assigned geographic positioning is based on a formula that emphasizes population centers. For instance, the city of Seattle will have 21 stores, Spokane will have eight and Pullman will have three.

There will be a 25% excise tax applied to every transaction on each level of the I-502 regulatory system: from producer to processor, processor to retailer, and retailer to customer. Local retail sales taxes are also applied to each purchase.

The official "Fiscal Impact Statement on I-502" report projects that legalization could deliver a stunning $2 billion in tax revenue to state coffers over the next five fiscal years. Tax revenue collected from legal cannabis sales in Washington will be earmarked for a dedicated fund, with the revenue being allocated for health care (55%), drug abuse treatment and education (25%), and marijuana-related research at University of Washington and Washington State University (1%). The remaining revenue will go towards the state general fund.

Washington and Colorado have both invested an enormous amount of time and resources in creating these systems. Multiple stakeholders from a variety of sectors contributed to their development. Each state spent over a year researching, analyzing and debating the issue in order to come up with these two distinctly different blueprints for legalization.

Cultivation facilities, product manufacturing facilities, testing facilities, and retail stores are now totally regulated and licensed in both states. Hundreds of millions of dollars will be added to local and state budgets each year. More importantly, citizens and visitors can finally enjoy this amazing plant in peace, without the creeping fear of getting nabbed by the police.

These two extraordinary ballot initiatives have seemingly paved the way for the rest of the country. So what happens next?

Cannabis still remains illegal on a federal level and federal law trumps all, regardless of what voters in Colorado, Washington or any of the other 48 states decide at the ballot box. Since everyone involved in the "legal cannabis" industry is defying federal laws against possessing the plant, we have created a bizarre predicament for several state employees in Colorado and Washington, who are technically laundering cash from "illegal drug sales" in the eyes of Uncle Sam.

When it comes to marijuana in the United States, it's no longer a question of 'when' or 'if', but 'how' it will be legalized.

We have two clear choices:

1. Continue this ponderous state-by-state process over the next 15 to 20 years (which is simply delaying the inevitable).
2. The federal government takes bold action now and legalizes cannabis for all uses from coast-to-coast.

U.S. States with Legal Medical Marijuana

"Is it rational to forbid patients who are dying from taking marijuana as a palliative to permit them to gain body weight and to get some food down? It seems madness to say, 'We're worried that they're going to become addicted to marijuana', when there's no evidence whatsoever that it's an addictive drug. But even if it were, these people are dying. What are we saving them from?"

- Cosmologist and Author **Carl Sagan**

A massive shift in public opinion over the past several years has dramatically accelerated the trend towards the complete legalization of medical marijuana nationwide.

Medical cannabis is already legal in 23 states (plus the District of Columbia). Unfortunately, many of these states have passed laws that are so restrictive it's virtually impossible for anyone to receiver for a prescription.

Medical marijuana laws and stipulations vary dramatically across the United States. Utah became the 21st state to approve medicinal cannabis in March 2014; however only children suffering from serious epileptic seizures can qualify for a prescription. No adults are allowed.

Several states have passed legislation similar to Utah, where the qualifying conditions are so narrow that only a tiny fraction of the overall patient population could ever hope to be approved.

The state of New Jersey might appear progressive at first glance, as they've had medical marijuana legislation on the books since 2010. But their qualifying standards are so stringent that it's practically impossible for a patient to get accepted into the program.

New Jersey has a very specific list of qualifying illnesses for their medical cannabis program, including cancer, multiple sclerosis, muscular dystrophy and Lou Gehrig's disease. In the five years since this law went into effect, only 300 patients have been approved by N.J. to legally use medical cannabis.

Surely there are more than 300 people in the entire fucking state of New Jersey who might benefit from medical cannabis. But unless your illness is on the list and Governor Chris Christie personally rubberstamps your application, you can spend the next few years in the state penitentiary for the heinous crime of trying to get healthy.

California, the first state to legalize medical marijuana back in 1996, has by far the least restrictive laws in the nation. According to the California Compassionate Use Act, physicians can write a prescription for "any illness" for which marijuana provides relief.

While the other 22 medical cannabis-friendly states require mandatory registration with the government, registration is completely voluntary for patients in California. There are over 550,000 people with active physician recommendations in this state of 38.3 million residents, which means California's population of approved medical marijuana patients is roughly equivalent to the entire state population of Wyoming.

Thousands of Americans who are suffering from serious illnesses are now seriously considering moving to a different state, just so they can have legal access to a variety of cannabis products and use them without fear of arrest.

Patients who cannot relocate to a medical marijuana friendly state only have three choices:

1. Break the law and risk arrest by using their medicine of choice
2. Switch to more dangerous pharmaceutical drugs
3. Accept their cruel fate and suffer in pain

What kind of a nation forces sick people to choose between these three terrible outcomes? It is ethically wrong to put families in this predicament. Patients with serious health issues don't have the finances, energy or emotional strength to move out of state and leave their friends and family behind.

No one suffering from pain should be forced to move across country just to get legal access to their preferred medicine of choice. But that's exactly what's happening right now.

This insanity cannot continue any longer.

The United States must legalize marijuana in 2015.

U.S. States that have Legalized Medical Marijuana:

- Alaska
- Arizona
- California
- Colorado
- Connecticut
- Delaware
- District of Columbia (Washington, D.C.)
- Hawaii
- Illinois
- Maine
- Maryland
- Massachusetts
- Michigan
- Montana
- Nevada
- New Hampshire

- New Jersey
- New Mexico
- Oregon
- Rhode Island
- Utah
- Vermont
- Washington

U.S. States with Legislation or Ballot Measures to Legalize Medical Marijuana in 2015

- Alabama
- Florida
- Iowa
- Missouri
- Nebraska
- Pennsylvania
- South Carolina
- Tennessee
- Texas

U.S. States with Legal Recreational Marijuana

On November 6, 2012, voters in Colorado and Washington approved measures to legalize, regulate and tax marijuana. This unprecedented legislation crystallized the enormous shift in public opinion currently taking place in America.

U.S. States that have legalized Recreational Cannabis

- Colorado (2014)
- Washington (2014)
- Oregon (effective July 1, 2015)
- Alaska (effective January 1, 2016)

It's truly a landmark moment in the cannabis movement when any adult in the world can visit Colorado and legally buy weed. But in the eyes of Uncle Sam, it doesn't really matter what the voters in Colorado, Oregon, Alaska and Washington have already decided at the ballot box. The DEA still considers marijuana a totally illegal, highly dangerous, Schedule I drug with absolutely no medical value, which puts these four states and their combined 17 million residents in direct opposition with the federal government.

Nothing is stopping the DEA from raiding legitimate cannabis businesses in Colorado tomorrow morning. The DEA does not operate by normal rules when it comes to search and seizure. Right now a bunch of agents could take a battering ram through the front door of any greenhouse or dispensary in Colorado (as they have already done several times this decade in California), barge in with guns raised high, and totally terrify the staff and customers. They can confiscate all the plants, medicine, cash and equipment in the building, and do it all without a warrant. These shadowy tactics should be considered unconstitutional behavior. Our taxes should not be providing billions of dollars to an agency that threatens to raid state-regulated cannabis operations.

The voters in four states have spoken. Cannabis should be taxed and regulated just like alcohol. Instead of interfering with this grand experiment, Uncle Sam should just buckle down and take some notes.

The United States needs to legalize marijuana in 2015.

Public Opinion is Rapidly Shifting

"Every age and generation must be as free to act for itself, in all cases, as the ages and generations which preceded it."

- **Thomas Paine**, *Common Sense* (1776)

The percentage of Americans in favor of marijuana legalization has skyrocketed over the past several years. This positive acceleration seems to be picking up new momentum with each political election.

Recent statistics show that across all demographics and political affiliations, Americans are finally beginning to understand that any perceived benefits we get from keeping cannabis illegal are greatly eclipsed by the tremendous costs associated with enforcing our feeble laws.

A survey conducted by the Pew Research Center in 2013 found that 72% of Americans think that government efforts to enforce current marijuana laws aren't worth the cost and drain on public resources. That same Pew survey showed over 52% of Americans voicing their support for complete marijuana legalization.

Back in the Eighties when the "war on drugs" was in full-on attack mode, only 16% of the U.S. population was in favor of legalization, while more than 70% of the U.S. population thought that smoking marijuana was morally wrong.

Fast forward to 2014, where a CNN/ORC survey revealed that only 35% of Americans think using cannabis is morally wrong, while a 55% majority indicated they were in favor of legalization. That is a stunning shift in public opinion over a 25 year period.

Millions of Americans will continue using marijuana for medical and recreational purposes, regardless of its legal status. Voters have finally realized that prosecuting citizens for possessing marijuana is a colossal waste of our nation's time and tax dollars. How long will it take our elected officials to arrive at the same conclusion?

Our federal government must abolish our nation's archaic marijuana laws in 2015 and support the rights of each individual state to create their own regulatory system.

The United States must legalize marijuana in 2015.

President Obama's Thoughts on Legalization

"Prohibition... goes beyond the bounds of reason in that it attempts to control mans' appetite through legislation and makes a crime out of things that are not even crimes... A prohibition law strikes a blow at the very principles upon which our Government was founded."

- President **Abraham Lincoln** (December 1840)

The Obama administration has sent mixed messages on cannabis during the president's two terms, creating a cloud of uncertainty over state-sanctioned medical marijuana sales that now transpire in nearly half of the 50 states. The official White House position on marijuana legalization is that it endangers public health "by increasing availability of drugs and undermining prevention activities."

A few days after Colorado and Washington voters legalized recreational marijuana in November 2012, Mr. Obama sat down with ABC's Barbara Walters, who asked the president how the United States government would react to this clear violation of federal law.

President Obama replied that law enforcement officials "have bigger fish to fry" and "it would not make sense for us to see a top priority as going after recreational users in states that have determined that it's legal."

This was an encouraging statement for proponents of legalization, but it pales in comparison to the media attention generated from an interview Mr. Obama conducted with David Remnick in the January 27, 2014 issue of the New Yorker, where the president softened his stance on cannabis.

Marijuana activists viewed President Obama's comments as a bellwether for the eventual decriminalization of marijuana on a federal level.

<u>President Obama's Thoughts on Marijuana Legalization:</u>

- "As has been well documented, I smoked pot as a kid, and I view it as a bad habit and a vice, not very different from the cigarettes that I smoked as a young person up through a big chunk of my adult life. I don't think it is more dangerous than alcohol."

- "We should not be locking up kids or individual users for long stretches of jail time when some of the folks who are writing those laws have probably done the same thing."

- "Middle-class kids don't get locked up for smoking pot, and poor kids do. And African-American kids and Latino kids are more likely to be poor and less likely to have the resources and the support to avoid unduly harsh penalties."

- Regarding legalization of marijuana in Colorado and Washington, Obama said, "it's important for it to go forward because it's important for society not to have a situation in which a large portion of people have at one time or another broken the law and only a select few get punished."

The quote that garnered the most media coverage was Obama's assertion that he didn't think marijuana is more dangerous than alcohol.

The argument that cannabis is a less dangerous alternative to alcohol was a huge catalyst for the legalization movement in Colorado, which was spearheaded by the Safer Alternative For Enjoyable Recreation (SAFER). This organization was founded on the principle that "Marijuana is safer than alcohol. It's time we treat it that way".

Last year a CNN survey revealed that nearly 75% of Americans believe alcohol is more dangerous than cannabis. Ask any police officer or emergency room doctor whether alcohol or marijuana creates more problems in our society, and they will unanimously agree that alcohol is by far the more dangerous drug.

So let's recap, shall we? The President of the United States says marijuana is less dangerous than alcohol, as do the vast majority of Americans. Yet alcohol is legally sold on practically every street corner in America, while a person smoking a joint is considered to be committing a federal offense.

If the American people and the President of the United States both agree that marijuana is less harmful than alcohol, why do we still have these outdated laws that encourage people to consume a more dangerous drug?

The United States must legalize marijuana in 2015.

CHAPTER 5: AN ENORMOUS ECONOMIC WINDFALL

"See, if you look at the drug war from a purely economic point of view, the role of the government is to protect the drug cartel. That's literally true."

- Nobel prize-winning economist **Milton Friedman**

The cannabis industry will continue growing at an exponential rate in America over the next several years.

Hundreds of cottage industries revolving around cannabis will be established and thousands of new businesses, products and services will be created. We have already noted the billions of dollars that America would generate and save from legalization. However, the permanent addition of hundreds of thousands of new jobs to the labor market might prove to be the biggest economic benefit of all.

The end of marijuana prohibition will lead to an abundance of new career opportunities. Retail stores, greenhouses, manufacturing facilities and testing labs across Colorado have created tons of new jobs over the past two years. Thousands of Coloradans are now legitimately employed in a wide range of positions including budtender, cannabis chef, accountant, lab analyst, grower and trimmer.

The alcohol industry currently employs millions of people around the world, from bartenders and brewmasters to distributors and sales people. The cannabis industry could also provide hundreds of thousands of people with a new career. But there's one distinct difference. The folks in the cannabis industry would feel much better about the product they were selling compared to the people pushing addictive spirits.

Marijuana is projected to become an $8.2 billion industry by 2018 through retail sales in Colorado, Washington, Oregon, Alaska and the 23 states with legal medical cannabis. However, this $8.2 billion figure is based strictly on legally generated revenue. The actual market for marijuana in the United States is much, much larger.

According to the groundbreaking June 2005 report "The Budgetary Implications of Marijuana Prohibition" by Jeffrey A. Miron, a senior fellow at the Cato Institute and Director of Undergraduate Studies in the Department of Economics at Harvard University, the illegal U.S. marijuana market has an estimated overall retail value of $113 billion.

This landmark study, which was co-signed by over 500 economists, concluded that the economic implications of legalizing marijuana in the U.S. would be immediate, massive and profound. Miron analyzed the costs of prohibition and projected that the United States could realize anywhere from $10 to $14 billion in annual savings and revenues if marijuana was regulated and taxed.

The financial figures involved are truly mind-blowing.

Economic Projections from Jeffrey A. Miron's "The Budgetary Implications of Marijuana Prohibition"

- **$7.7 billion** in government expenses would be saved annually on prohibition enforcement. State and Local governments would reap $5.3 billion of this savings, while the federal government would accrue $2.4 billion.
- **$2.4 billion** in tax revenue would be generated each year if marijuana were legalized and taxed like all other goods.
- **$6.2 billion** in tax revenue would be generated annually if marijuana were taxed at rates similar to alcohol and tobacco products.
- **$10.7 billion** is spent annually on arresting people for marijuana.

While considering these figures, it's important to remember the total U.S. federal debt has mushroomed to a stunning $18.1 trillion. Since our nation is **$18 trillion** in debt, bold and decisive action is required to raise capital, reduce debt and return our nation's budget back to positive integers.

If a family or business is facing a negative bank balance, there are only two options moving forward: generate more cash or reduce spending. Legalizing marijuana would let us take both courses of action simultaneously.

From an economic point of view, the true beauty of marijuana legalization is that the financial benefits would be doubled. Billions would be generated through taxes on marijuana transactions, and billions would be saved in law enforcement, legal and correctional resources.

Millions of lives have been ruined by America's brutal and inhumane campaign against marijuana users and growers. Billions of dollars are wasted each year on arresting and jailing cannabis users. This is a colossal waste of our law enforcement, prosecution and prison resources.

The war against marijuana is over. The final score was Marijuana - Infinity, United States - Zero. Many historians have labeled it the biggest ass-kicking in history. Despite being defeated and driven back by mighty marijuana on the battlefields of America, the federal government continues to act there are still a couple ticks left on the clock.

Not only are we losing billions of dollars fighting this futile war against marijuana, we have created an underground market that funnels enormous profits to the drug cartels and street gangs who import and sell cannabis.

Based on reports from the Library of Congress, the Office of National Drug Control Policy and other government sources, the annual supply of marijuana in America is estimated to be 31 million pounds. At an average retail price of $7.87 per gram and an average tax rate of 28.7%, tax revenue produced from marijuana sales should easily top $30 billion annually by 2020.

Imagine how many schools, bridges, roads, parks and community projects could be funded from taxing and regulating cannabis!

The decision to end the war on cannabis right now would not cost a single penny. Instead it would redirect billions of dollars from the underworld into our local communities and totally improve our quality of life.

What the heck are we waiting for?

The United States must legalize marijuana in 2015.

CHAPTER 6: A MULTITUDE OF MEDICAL BENEFITS

"It is intellectually dishonest to say it has no value whatsoever, because it's just not true."

- **Dr. Igor Grant**, Director of the University of California's Center for Medicinal Cannabis Research

Of all the herbs, plants, shrubs and trees that God placed on our beautiful green Earth, it is cannabis that offers the widest range of mental and physical health benefits. The potential of cannabis to treat such a diverse array of medical issues should be ample enough reason to justify the complete legalization of marijuana in the USA right now. If the Federal Government truly cared about the well-being of the American, it would end marijuana prohibition immediately, simply to give patients legal access to a safer, more effective and less addictive drug than any poisonous pill produced by Big Pharma.

Millions of legally registered marijuana patients across the USA have already experienced the medical wonders of cannabis. For Americans who are seeking a less toxic and harmful way to reduce their stress or alleviate chronic pain, this herb is nothing short of a miracle drug.

Patients who are recovering from chemotherapy or fighting wasting syndrome due to the ravages of AIDS or cancer can testify that marijuana is incredibly effective when it comes to stimulating appetites and relieving nausea. Cannabis reduces ocular pressure in glaucoma patients and helps prevent blindness. It is a godsend for anyone who suffers from debilitating migraine headaches. And the anti-epileptic properties of cannabis have been proven to dramatically reduce the muscle spasticity that accompanies cerebral palsy and multiple sclerosis.

The flowering buds of female cannabis plants contain more than 400 chemicals. This includes more than 60 known cannabinoids, which are the active compounds unique to marijuana. Dozens of active cannabinoids contain chemical compounds with homoeopathic traits, including Cannabidiol, Cannabichromene and Tetrahydrocannabiuarin.

Several of the cannabinoids found in marijuana are psychoactive, with delta-9-tetrahydrocannabinol (THC) being the most commonly known amongst casual cannabis users. THC delivers psychoactive effects that provide uplifting and euphoric sensations which can help relieve stress and depression.

The important thing to remember when contemplating the possibilities of medical cannabis is that dried plant matter doesn't need to be smoked. It can be eaten, vaporized, delivered through a transdermal patch or converted into a spray that you squirt under your tongue. All of these delivery methods eliminate all the toxic byproducts that come from inhaling smoke.

The University of California's Center for Medicinal Cannabis Research (CMCR) was established by the California state legislature in 2010. The CMCR was granted three years to conduct rigorous scientific studies in order to determine the safety and efficacy of cannabis for treating medical conditions.

After three years of intensive medical research, the CMCR concluded there is "reasonable evidence that cannabis is a promising treatment in selected pain syndromes caused by injury or diseases of the nervous system."

Neuropsychiatrist Dr. Igor Grant, who served as director of the CMCR, said that, "Every one of the studies showed a benefit. The convergence of evidence makes me convinced there is a medical benefit here, and there may be a niche for cannabis."

Dr. Grant stressed that marijuana's absurd classification as a Schedule I drug "is completely at odds with the existing science."

Without access to legal medical cannabis, patients are more likely to receive prescriptions for much more dangerous, expensive and addictive pharmaceutical drugs. The popularity of opiate-based prescription drugs is reverse-fueling an alarming resurgence in heroin, creating a deadly two-headed epidemic that shows absolutely no signs of slowing down.

Right now in America we are forcing good people to visit unsafe environments in order to acquire their medicine of choice. When you are forced into the black market, you are not only forced to deal with shady and nefarious characters, you are often limited to just one strain. People with conditions such as epilepsy or multiple sclerosis require strains that deliver certain medical properties. Under the current black market system it is nearly impossible for the average person to acquire a specific strain.

Scores of patients, doctors and researchers have vouched for the effectiveness of this plant in helping patients live heathier lives. Yet the federal government still insists that any citizen who chooses to use marijuana to treat their condition is committing a criminal act. It is barbaric and inhumane for our government to deny patients safe access to *any* medicine that might improve their condition.

The United States must legalize cannabis in 2015.

How can Cannabinoids benefit patients?

"Marijuana is the wonder drug of the future."

- **Dr. Lester Grinspoon**, Professor of Psychiatry at Harvard Medical School

The following is a list of known cannabinoids and their specific medical benefits. Most of this information is reprinted with permission from Steve Cottrell at AZMedTest.com, which is a state-of-the-art testing facility in Tempe, AZ offering medicinal cannabis testing for dispensaries and caregivers in Arizona.

Cannabidiol (CBD)

Out of all the components found in medical cannabis, Cannabidiol (CBD) has been found to deliver the most medical benefits. CBD has strong antioxidant properties and has been hailed as a "miracle drug" by patients suffering from epileptic seizures.

Studies have shown CBD's specific medicinal values:

- Helps control certain cancers
- Helps with controlling pain
- Stimulates bone growth
- Stops growth of bacteria
- Suppresses muscle spasms and convulsions
- Slows Inflammation
- Helps with nausea
- Reduces the risk of artery obstructions
- Decreases pressure in the blood vessel walls
- Reduces blood sugar levels
- Assists in controlling epileptic seizures
- Helps reduce risk of nerve damage
- Decreases the social isolation caused by THC

Tetrahydrocannabinol (THC)

THC is associated with a wide range of medical and mood-altering benefits. It is most frequently connected with the "high" and uplifting feelings that accompany cannabis use. THC has very high psychoactive characteristics, typically ranging from 5 to 25 percent. Over-medicating with THC can sometimes cause adverse side effects.

Studies have shown THC's specific medicinal values:

- Helps with controlling pain
- Helps with relaxation
- Suppresses pain from nerve damage
- Helps reduce risk of nerve damage
- Helps control anxiety
- Suppresses muscle spasms and convulsions
- Helps control certain cancers
- Helps with nausea
- Slows inflammation
- Helps fight free radicals in the blood stream
- Encourages eating and appetite stimulation
- Stimulates new growth in nerve tissue
- Relieves chronic eye pressure and pain caused from glaucoma and other eye disorders

Cannabinol (CBN)

There is very little Cannabinol present in fresh marijuana plants. Medical cannabis containing high levels of CBN conversely has very low levels of THC. High levels of CBN may indicate that the plants were improperly handled or cured.

High levels of CBN have been shown to cause undesirable symptoms like confusion or lightheadedness.

Studies have shown CBN's specific medicinal values:

- Acts as a sleep aid
- Slows inflammation
- Helps with controlling pain
- Suppresses muscle spasms and convulsions
- Helps fight free radicals in the blood stream

Cannabichromene (CBC)

Very little is known about CBC, but preliminary research has been very promising. CBC has no known psychoactive characteristics associated to it.

Studies have shown CBC's specific medicinal values:

- Helps with controlling pain
- Stops growth of Fungi
- Slows inflammation
- Stimulates bone growth
- Encourages cell growth
- Stops growth of bacteria
- Assists in contraction of blood cells

CHAPTER 7: INDICA & SATIVA – CANNABIS STRAINS WITH DIFFERENT EFFECTS

"I think people need to be educated to the fact that marijuana is not a drug. Marijuana is an herb and a flower. God put it here. If He put it here and He wants it to grow, what gives the government the right to say that God is wrong?"

- Country music legend **Willie Nelson**

An important message to anyone who has only tried marijuana once or twice and didn't really care for it: the information contained in this chapter might totally change your life.

People who have never tried marijuana before usually associate it with worn-out stereotypes of the "stoner" sitting on the couch, eating Doritos and playing video games. These people are obviously not familiar with the dramatic psychoactive differences between indica and sativa flowers.

During my early days experimenting with marijuana, there's no way my research would have continued much further if I had only been exposed to indica strains. I personally prefer the energetic, uplifting and cerebral high that comes from sativa strains. I never really bother much with indica strains unless I need help falling asleep.

However, a shocking number of casual (and even regular) cannabis consumers have absolutely no clue about the differences between indicas, sativas and hybrids. Moreover, they rarely have multiple choices when it comes to selecting a strain. Your friendly, neighborhood weed dealer usually only has a couple options to choose from, and the available product is more likely to be categorized with a street name describing its potency (such as Reggie, Mids, or the Fuckin' Bomb) rather than its genetics and actual strain name. Your typical street dealer is way more interested in money than botany, and thinks indica is a fancy name for the color blue.

Now it's time for a quick cannabis botany lesson.

There are three distinct species of marijuana: *Cannabis ruderalis*, *Cannabis indica* and *Cannabis sativa*.

Cannabis ruderalis is what's known as the "hemp" version of the plant. Hemp provides hundreds of useful items for humans, including food, clothing, rope, oil, paper and soap. But since hemp doesn't contain any psychoactive chemicals, it is impossible to get "high" from smoking it.

The other two species of marijuana, *Cannabis indica* and *Cannabis sativa*, are world-renowned and sought after by millions of humans for their mental and physical effects. You can most definitely get high from smoking or ingesting the flowers produced by indica and sativa plants.

Indica and sativa are both effective in relieving nausea and stimulating appetites, which is why both species are valuable for patients suffering from AIDS, cancer or recovering from chemotherapy. But when you compare the psychoactive effects of *C. indica* and *C. sativa*, you'll find that they deliver dramatically different effects to the user.

Every strain of cannabis that is grown for medical or recreational consumption can be classified as an indica strain, a sativa strain or a hybrid of both. There are hundreds of different strains to choose from and each has its own unique attributes. The appearance, smell, stickiness, flowering time, height and bud size can vary dramatically between two strains. More crucially, the psychoactive traits of each indica, sativa or hybrid strain can deliver markedly different effects.

Many of the top-selling strains in the United States are hybrids. Hybrids are created when a cannabis botanist breeds together two strains, seeking certain characteristics of both indica and sativa. Since hybrids can help patients cope with multiple health issues simultaneously (such as relieving chronic pain while also reducing stress and anxiety), these strains are especially popular among patients in medical marijuana-friendly states.

Let's learn more about sativa, indica and hybrid strains, shall we?

Sativa Strains

Sativa strains deliver an uplifting, energetic and cerebral high which is ideal for daytime smoking, socializing and outdoor activity. Many people experience increased creative thinking and a heightened sense of awareness while under the influence of sativas, which is why these strains are preferred by writers, musicians, painters and anyone creating art.

Sativa strains offer an immediate antidote for miserable moods. If an independent research firm held a contest to determine which substance deserves the title of the "World's Greatest Anti-Depressant", I guarantee that sativa strains would beat the living shit out of Prozac, Abilify or any other pill that the prescription drug companies might enter in the competition.

Pills like Prozac and Abilify take several days (or even weeks) to reach their full effectiveness, but the effects of inhaling cannabis are practically instantaneous. Pharmaceutical companies readily admit that people who take their anti-depressants might experience some seriously scary side effects, including an increased risk of killing yourself.

Words like euphoria, elevating and energetic are frequently used to describe sativa strains, and there's no doubt that the United States would be a happier and healthier place if we replaced all synthetic anti-depressant medications with this natural wonder drug called *Cannabis sativa*.

Popular Sativa strains:

- Sour Diesel
- Jack Herer
- Durban Poison
- Purple Haze
- Green Crack
- Purple Diesel
- Super Silver Haze

Indica Strains

Indica strains provide a relaxing, overall body high which is tremendously beneficial for patients who are experiencing muscle spasms, seizures, migraine headaches, chronic pain or sleeping disorders.

For people suffering from unbearable conditions like fibromyalgia and Multiple Sclerosis, pure indica strains can truly act as a wonder drug.

Popular Indica strains:

- Northern Lights
- Bubba Kush
- God's Gift
- Cheese
- Skywalker
- Purple Kush
- Granddaddy Purple
- Afghan Kush
- G-13

Hybrid Strains

"Why is marijuana against the law? It grows naturally upon our planet. Doesn't the idea of making nature against the law seem to you a bit… unnatural?"

- Comedian **Bill Hicks**

Many of the top-selling strains in the United States are hybrid strains, which offer a combination of effects from both psychoactive species. Hybrids are created when a cannabis breeder seeking specific genetic traits selects two different strains and breeds them together, hoping that the resulting offspring will boast the strongest characteristics of its two parent plants.

Someone suffering from chronic pain and depression might be having a tough time just getting out of bed. An educated, compassionate doctor could recommend a hybrid cannabis strain such "Girl Scout Cookies", which has a high THC content of 18-23% and is a cross between three different types of strains:

- Durban Poison (sativa)
- OG Kush (hybrid)
- Cherry Kush (hybrid)

Patient reviews on the popular cannabis strain review website Leafly.com show the top three medical benefits of Girl Scout Cookies are:

- o Relieving pain
- o Relieving stress
- o Relieving depression

Never will you find a person in severe pain who is feeling happy and relaxed. People suffering from serious pain can often get stressed out and sad about their current state. It's tough to smile when you are experiencing anxiety over medical bills and possibly facing your own mortality. Anyone who is suffering from serious physical pain or mental anguish should strongly consider experimenting with a few hybrids to see if this miraculous plant can help alleviate their distress.

It's not hyperbole to call hybrid strains a miracle drug. Hybrids can help patients fight pain, stress and depression - all at the same time.

Popular Hybrid strains:

- Acapulco Gold
- OG Kush
- Blue Dream
- Headband
- Girl Scout Cookies
- Pineapple Express

- White Widow
- Chemdawg

CHAPTER 8: DELIVERING A SERIOUS BLOW TO DRUG CARTELS

"See, if you look at the drug war from a purely economic point of view, the role of the government is to protect the drug cartel. That's literally true."

- Nobel Prize-winning economist **Milton Friedman**

Legalization would deliver a serious blow to Mexican drug cartels, who generate a substantial amount of their income from importing cannabis into the United States. Experts believe that drug cartel revenues would drop by at least 50% if cannabis prohibition laws were abolished.

Several prominent leaders of nations south of the border are publically campaigning for the outright legalization of marijuana, including the presidents of Colombia (Juan Manuel Santos), Guatemala (Otto Perez Molina) and Uruguay (José Alberto "Pepe" Mujica). One of the most vocal proponents of legalization is the former president of Mexico, Vicente Fox, who witnessed soaring levels of violence and corruption revolving around the trafficking of cannabis and other drugs during his six years in office from 2000 to 2006.

An increasing number of criminal justice industry professionals in the U.S. are vocally supporting this pragmatic solution proposed by Latin American leaders, despite the very strong likelihood of facing scorn and resentment from their colleagues.

Many police officers already recognize that the 'war on drugs' is impossible to win. Intelligent cops realize that if the ultimate goal of marijuana prohibition is the complete eradication of cannabis, you might as well call every cop "Officer Sisyphus".

Sensible people from the front lines of America's drug war have banded together to form a nonprofit organization called **Law Enforcement Against Prohibition**. LEAP is comprised of smart police officers who recognize that arresting citizens for a harmless, victimless crime is colossal waste of everyone's time.

Mission Statement of LEAP:

> "Our experience on the front lines of the 'War on Drugs' has led us to call for a repeal of prohibition and its replacement with a tight system of legalized regulation, which will effectively cripple the violent cartels and street dealers who control the current illegal market."

That sounds pretty logical, right? Just legalize cannabis today and the black market vanishes tomorrow. Then our police officers can focus their efforts on catching criminals who commit serious offenses like robbery, rape and assault. After all, doesn't it seem rather preposterous for a cop to stop and arrest someone for the trivial crime of smoking weed, when he could be pursuing a violent thief, rapist or murderer?

The United States cannot proceed with business as usual. The bad guys will keep earning billions while we spend billions trying to catch them. We made the rules of this game, and the game is rigged in favor of the cartels. It's impossible to win from an economic perspective. Now it's time to change the rules.

The United States government has the power to permanently put all the criminals who are trafficking illegal marijuana out of business, while simultaneously delivering a serious setback to the deadly drug cartels.

The biggest secret about the 'War on Drugs', and more specifically the 'War on Cannabis' is that **America can stop this war right now without spending a dime or lifting a finger**.

The net positives for our society and our nation would vastly outweigh any perceived downsides.

The United States must legalize cannabis in 2015.

CHAPTER 9: THE LIFE ENHANCING EFFECTS OF MARIJUANA

"The illegality of cannabis is outrageous, an impediment to full utilization of a drug which helps produce the serenity and insight, sensitivity and fellowship so desperately needed in this increasingly mad and dangerous world."

- Cosmologist **Carl Sagan**

People enjoy marijuana on a recreational basis for one simple reason. It brings them genuine pleasure.

When you are feeling glum and depressed, cannabis can give you a swift happy kick in the ass and wash your blues away in seconds. Cannabis enhances and deepens the pleasure of music, nature and sex. Cannabis can inspire you to try new things like yoga, cooking, painting, gardening and playing the guitar.

Let me introduce you to a gentleman named Dr. Lester Grinspoon, who was professor of psychiatry emeritus at Harvard Medical School and author of the book *Marijuana Reconsidered*. This brilliant man was also a senior psychiatrist at the Massachusetts Mental Health Center in Boston for over four decades.

Dr. Grinspoon held a strong bias against cannabis when he first began studying the plant's effects on humans. Like many Americans, he had been deceived by government propaganda that portrayed cannabis as a dangerous drug with absolutely no medical value.

As Dr. Grinspoon began conducting his research and his knowledge grew deeper, he started his own first-hand experiments with the plant. Soon his previously-held viewpoints against marijuana not only melted away, they were completely reversed. The good doctor found cannabis safe to use and also incredibly beneficial for the pure enjoyment of life.

This Ivy League professor was shocked to find that his previously held beliefs were completely backwards. "Much to my astonishment, here I was trained in science and medicine and had to discover that I had been brainwashed like just about every other American," said Grinspoon. "Once I was convinced that it was safe, and satisfied my curiosity about it, it took me a number of years to realize what a remarkable substance it was."

According to Dr. Grinspoon, there are three categories of cannabis use: medical, recreational and enhancement. We've discussed the first two categories, medical and recreational, at length throughout this book.

But it's the third category, a phenomenon that Dr. Grinspoon called "enhancement", that is difficult to for people who have never partaken in nature's miracle plant to understand.

The mainstream media currently classifies cannabis consumption as being either medical or recreational, but Grinspoon says "that is hardly an adequate description of, say, marijuana's capacity to catalyze ideas and insights, heighten the appreciation of music and art, or deepen emotional and sexual intimacy."

Marijuana can help you rediscover the wonders of nature and deepen your appreciation for the immensity of the universe. Many religious groups use cannabis as a sacred part of their spiritual growth, and feel that it helps bring people closer together.

We have presented many valid reasons to legalize cannabis over the course of this book. But the "enhancing" effects of cannabis, and potential to raise our nation's collective conscience, break down barriers and bring our communities closer together, might be the powerful reason of all for the United States to legalize cannabis in 2015.

CHAPTER 10: CONCLUSION

"To reason with governments, as they have existed for ages, is to argue with brutes. It is only from the nations themselves that reforms can be expected."

- **Thomas Paine**, *Common Sense* (1776)

Ladies and gentlemen of the jury, you have just been presented with hundreds of compelling reasons why my client should be let go from the shackles she has been unjustly bound in for the past 76 years.

Cannabis gives us food, medicine and fun times. It was put on this beautiful green Earth to help human beings. Yet the United States government continues to arrest anyone who dares associate with her.

The primary danger for marijuana users in America is getting caught with it. Americans have a greater fear of the police than the plant itself, and they should. People get beat up and abused by power-hungry police all the time. But history shows that cannabis has never instigated a fight, and there has never been a fatality directly associated with marijuana. No one has ever overdosed. It's physically impossible.

America's oppressive marijuana laws have no moral basis or credibility. It is reprehensible for our government to reject countless testimonials from patients who have personally experienced the medical miracles of cannabis.

If the Federal Government truly cares about the well-being, liberty and freedom of the citizens, we need to regulate tax and legalize cannabis NOW and immediately stop prosecuting patients, jailing peaceful people and ruining lives.

There are thousands of reasons why the United States should legalize cannabis in 2015. Coming up with an explanation to justify keeping it illegal is practically impossible. There is no reason to wait any longer.

The United States must legalize marijuana in 2015.

EPILOGUE

"Y ou may be 38 years old, as I happen to be. And one day, some great opportunity stands before you and calls you to stand up for some great principle, some great issue, some great cause…

…and you refuse to do it because you are afraid.

You refuse to do it because you want to live longer. You're afraid that you will lose your job, or you are afraid that you will be criticized or that you will lose your popularity, or you're afraid that somebody will stab you, or shoot at you or bomb your house; so you refuse to take the stand.

Well, you may go on and live until you are 90, but you're just as dead at 38 as you would be at 90. And the cessation of breathing in your life is but the belated announcement of an earlier death of the spirit."

- The Reverend Dr. Martin Luther King, Jr.

GET INVOLVED AND TAKE ACTION NOW

- **NORML.org** - Founded in 1970, the National Organization for the Reform of Marijuana Laws is a non-profit organization based in Washington, DC that has been fighting for the legalization of recreational marijuana in the United States longer than any other organization.

- **SaferChoice.org** - SAFER's mission is to educate the public about the relative safety of marijuana compared to alcohol. This organization was a huge factor in getting cannabis legalized in Colorado.

- **MPP.org** - Marijuana Policy Project. Founded in January 1995, this lobbyist group headquartered in Washington, DC is fighting for the rights of medical marijuana patients, lobbying for legislation and sponsoring ballot initiatives to replace marijuana prohibition with a sensible system of regulation

- **DrugPolicy.org** - The Drug Policy Alliance (DPA) is the nation's leading organization promoting drug policies that are grounded in science, compassion, health and human rights.

- **ACLU.org/criminal-law-reform/marijuana-law-reform** – The American Civil Liberties Union's marijuana law reform page. The Criminal Law Reform Project advocates for the decriminalization of personal possession of marijuana across the nation.

GET EDUCATED:

- **Jackherer.com/thebook/** - Free online version of *The Emperor Wears No Clothes* by legendary cannabis freedom fighter Jack Herer. This is the best-selling marijuana book of all time, written by one of the most influential figures in the history of modern marijuana. Herer was so confident in the bullet-proof research he conducted for *The Emperor Wears No Clothes*, he boldly offered a $100,000 reward to anyone who could refute a single fact in this book. Over 700,000 copies of *The Emperor Wears No Clothes* have been sold around the world since the first edition was published in 1985, and Herer has yet to pay a single dime in reward money.

- **EdRosenthal.com** – Homepage of Ed Rosenthal, the 'Guru of Ganja' and an iconic figure in the history of modern cannabis. Mr. Rosenthal is a legendary cannabis horticulturist and prolific author of a dozen books that have sold over one million copies combined.

- **RxMarijuana.com** – This website is devoted to the exchange of information about the use of marijuana as a medicine. It was launched by Dr. Lester Grinspoon, Associate Professor of Psychiatry (Emeritus) at Harvard Medical School and James Bakalar, J.D. of the Department of Psychiatry at Harvard Medical School as a place to learn about patients' experiences with medical marijuana.

- **Marijuana-uses.com** – Another website launched by Dr. Lester Grinspoon, this one features over 100 personal essays, testimonials and endorsements from cannabis enthusiasts.

- **CSDP.org** – Common Sense for Drug Policy is a nonprofit organization dedicated to reforming drug policy and expanding harm reduction.

- **HighTimes.com** – Founded in 1974, this New York-based magazine and website is devoted to the legalization of cannabis.

- **MedicalMarijuana.procon.org** - ProCon.org is a nonprofit public charity. Their purpose is to provide resources for critical thinking and to educate without bias.

- **Drugwarfacts.org** - Since it first went online in 1998, Drug War Facts provides reliable information with applicable citations on important public health and criminal justice issues.

- **DrugLibrary.org** – The Schaffer Library of Drug Policy has extensive historical documents and archives that show marijuana prohibition was built on lies and deceit.

- **StoptheDrugWar.org** - StoptheDrugWar.org works for an end to drug prohibition worldwide, and an end to the "drug war" in its current form.

- **Leafly.com** – The world's largest cannabis strain resource with an extensive directory of medical dispensaries.

- **WeedMaps.com** – Comprehensive directory of medical marijuana dispensaries, doctors and delivery services.

- **CMCR.UCSD.EDU** – Home of the University of California's Center for Medicinal *Cannabis Research* (CMCR). Their mission is to coordinate rigorous scientific studies to assess the safety and efficacy of cannabis and cannabis compounds for treating medical conditions.

- **CannabisCulture.com** – Vancouver-based website covering the cannabis industry and culture.

- **MikuriyaMedical.com/about/can_write.html** – Articles and research from Dr. Tod H. Mikuriya, who is considered to be the grandfather of the medical Cannabis movement. Dr. Mikuriya was a psychiatrist and staunch advocate for the legalization of the use of marijuana for medical purposes.

- **MikuriyaMedical.com/about/cw_alcsub**.pdf - PDF version of influential research study "Cannabis as a Substitute for Alcohol: A Harm-Reduction Approach" by Dr. Tod H. Mikuriya

CONTACT ELECTED OFFICIALS:

U.S. Senators:

Senate.gov/contacting/index_by_state.cfm

U.S. Representatives:

House.gov/representatives/

State Governors:

Usa.gov/Contact/Governors.shtml

State Legislators:

Thomas.loc.gov/home/state-legislatures.html

Find contact information for all state and federal elected officials and U.S. government agencies at: www.usa.gov/Contact/Elected.shtml

FEEDBACK AND FUTURE EDITIONS

Dear Readers,

We plan on releasing updated editions of Cannabis Sense each and every year until marijuana is legalized by the federal government.

If you have any feedback, suggestions or content ideas for next year's edition of *Cannabis Sense*, I would love to hear from you. Feel free to contact me at derekdwilliams@gmail.com.

Nothing is more powerful than a personal testimonial when it comes to kicking the truth about cannabis. If your life has been impacted in a positive way by cannabis and you want to share your experience, please contact me. We may include your story in future editions of the book or feature it on our website CannabisSenseAmerica.com.

Thanks for reading *Cannabis Sense 2015*, and please get involved with the marijuana legalization movement today. Your fellow Americans are counting on you.

Love,

Derek

Notes and References

CHAPTER ONE: "The Anti-Marijuana Faction is Driven by Fear and Loathing"

- http://blog.sfgate.com/smellthetruth/2014/01/21/cnns-insane-clown-nancy-grace-converts-millions-to-marijuana-legalization/

- http://piersmorgan.blogs.cnn.com/2014/01/23/ann-coulter-on-potheads-they-cant-perform-any-useful-jobs/

- http://www.huffingtonpost.com/2014/01/23/ann-coulter-pot-economy-piers-morgan_n_4650921.html

- http://www.famousscientists.org/14-famous-scientists-inventors-who-experimented-with-drugs/

- http://www.huffingtonpost.com/2013/09/18/famous-marijuana-users_n_3948855.html

"America's Longtime Commissioner of Narcotics was a Racist Lunatic"

http://www.change.org/petitions/u-s-government-acknowledge-that-the-racism-of-harry-anslinger-led-to-cannabis-prohibition

http://www.pbs.org/wgbh/pages/frontline/shows/dope/etc/cron.html

http://www.britannica.com/blogs/2010/10/reefer-madness-and-the-prohibition-of-marijuana-in-- the-united-states/

http://www.hemp.org/news/book/export/html/626

http://www.drugwarrant.com/articles/why-is-marijuana-illegal/

http://www.hempology.org/

- http://reefermadnessmuseum.org/chap10/Gore.htm

- http://www.druglibrary.org/schaffer/hemp/taxact/taxact.htm

- http://www.csdp.org/publicservice/anslinger.htm

"America's Leading Expert on Marijuana Testified that Two Puffs Turned Him into a Bat"

- http://www.telegraph.co.uk/culture/books/3597114/After-two-puffs-I-was-turned-into-a-bat.html

- http://www.druglibrary.org/schaffer/hemp/taxact/munch2.htm

"Key Government Agencies Have Opposing Views on Cannabis"

- http://www.google.com/patents/US6630507

- http://nypost.com/2013/09/11/feds-patented-medical-marijuana-even-when-they-were-fighting-it/

- http://www.justice.gov/dea/

- http://www.justice.gov/dea/druginfo/ds.shtml

- http://www.justice.gov/dea/docs/dangers-consequences-marijuana-abuse.pdf

- http://www.justice.gov/dea/pr/multimedia-library/publications/speaking_out.pdf

- http://abcnews.go.com/Health/PainNews/marijuana-advocates-sue-feds-dea-rejects-weed-medicine/story?id=14046823

- http://www.deamuseum.org/ccp/index.html

- http://www.deamuseum.org/ccp/cannabis/effects.html

- http://www.zogenix.com/content/products/zohydro.htm

- http://www.cnn.com/2014/02/26/health/zohydro-approval/index.html?hpt=hp_t1

"Marijuana is Grown at Ole Miss and Legally Distributed by Uncle Sam"

- http://www.usatoday.com/story/news/nation/2012/12/28/medical-marijuana-lab-in-mississippi/1796475/

CHAPTER TWO:

"Big Alcohol"

http://www.ntsb.gov/news/events/2013/eliminate_impaired_driving/faq.html

- http://www.cdc.gov/brfss/

- http://archive.saferchoice.org/content/view/24/53/

- http://www.gallup.com/poll/141656/drinking-rate-edges-slightly-year-high.aspx

-
http://www.ntsb.gov/news/events/2013/eliminate_impaired_driving/faq.html

"Big Pharma"

- http://www.cdc.gov/homeandrecreationalsafety/overdose/facts.html

- http://www.cdc.gov/homeandrecreationalsafety/rxbrief/

- http://www.samhsa.gov/data/2k13/DataReview/DR006/nonmedical-pain-reliever-use-2013.htm

- http://rxmarijuana.com/articles.htm

- http://www.cnbc.com/id/36177544

- http://www.trutv.com/conspiracy/in-the-shadows/pot-illegal/big-pharma-government.html

"Big Tobacco"

- http://www.surgeongeneral.gov/initiatives/tobacco/

- http://www.surgeongeneral.gov/library/reports/50-years-of-progress/fact-sheet.html

- http://www.cancer.gov/cancertopics/pdq/cam/cannabis/patient/page1

- http://www.medicalnewstoday.com/releases/104949.php

- *The Health Consequences of Smoking—50 Years of Progress: A Report of the Surgeon General, 2014 | SurgeonGeneral.gov.* (n.d.). Retrieved January 17, 2014, from http://www.surgeongeneral.gov/library/reports/50-years-of-progress/index.html

"Police, Prosecutors and the Prison-Industrial Complex"

- http://www.cato.org/publications/white-paper/drug-decriminalization-portugal-lessons-creating-fair-successful-drug-policies

- http://www.rawstory.com/rs/2014/01/16/dea-official-freaks-out-at-senate-hearing-reckless-marijuana-legalization-scares-us/

"Partnership for a Drug-Free America"

- http://fair.org/extra-online-articles/pot-boiler/

- http://www.drugfree.org/drug-guide/marijuana

CHAPTER THREE:

Websites

- http://www.gallup.com/poll/165539/first-time-americans-favor-legalizing-marijuana.aspx

- http://liq.wa.gov/marijuana/I-502

- http://www.brookings.edu/research/papers/2013/05/21-legal-marijuana-colorado-washington

- http://www.bloomberg.com/news/2013-05-30/the-u-s-is-changing-its-mind-about-marijuana.html

- http://www.reuters.com/article/2014/04/11/us-colorado-marijuana-idUSBREA3A1X720140411

- https://www.moodys.com/research/Moodys-Colorados-tax-revenues-from-legalized-marijuana-exceeding-expectations--PR_297013

- http://www.time.com/time/health/article/0,8599,1931247,00.html

-
http://www.usatoday.com/story/news/nation/2014/04/09/recreational
-pot-sales-forecast-at-8-billion-a-year-by-2018/7513357/

- http://www.rollingstone.com/politics/pages/the-weed-issue-
marijuana-legalization-status-by-state-weedmap-20130610

"U.S. States with Legal Medical Cannabis"

- http://norml.org/

- http://www.canorml.org/medical-marijuana/patients-guide-to-
california-law

- http://www.state.nj.us/health/medicalmarijuana/faqs.shtml

-
http://medicalmarijuana.procon.org/view.answers.php?questionID=001
199

"U.S. States with Legal Recreational Cannabis"

- http://xcannabis.com/cannabis-news/news-and-archives-about-
washingtons-initiative-502/

-
http://www.sos.state.co.us/pubs/elections/Initiatives/titleBoard/filings
/2011-2012/30Final.pdf

-
http://www.nola.com/news/index.ssf/2014/01/so_many_seek_a_licens
e_to_grow.html

- http://www.king5.com/news/local/First-ever-pot-shop-lottery-kicks-off-in-WA-256021551.html

"Public Opinion is Rapidly Changing"

- http://www.bloomberg.com/news/2013-05-30/the-u-s-is-changing-its-mind-about-marijuana.html

- http://nation.time.com/2013/05/28/how-america-learned-to-stop-worrying-and-love-marijuana/

- http://www.brookings.edu/research/papers/2013/05/21-legal-marijuana-colorado-washington

- http://www.usatoday.com/story/news/nation/2014/01/20/marijuana-more-dangerous-alcohol-president-obama/4660555/

"President Obama's Thoughts on Legalization"

- http://www.whitehouse.gov/ondcp/marijuana

- http://www.whitehouse.gov/ondcp/ondcp-fact-sheets/marijuana-legalization

- http://www.newyorker.com/reporting/2014/01/27/140127fa_fact_remnick

- http://politicalticker.blogs.cnn.com/2014/01/07/cnn-poll-americans-say-marijuana-is-less-dangerous-than-booze-or-tobacco/

http://www.washingtonpost.com/blogs/post-politics/wp/2012/12/14/obama-ive-got-bigger-fish-to-fry-than-pot-smokers/

CHAPTER FOUR:

http://www.usatoday.com/story/news/nation/2014/04/09/recreational-pot-sales-forecast-at-8-billion-a-year-by-2018/7513357/

http://www.prohibitioncosts.org/

http://www.prohibitioncosts.org/mironreport/#sthash.qTT7OVWk.dpuf

http://www.prohibitioncosts.org/executive-summary/#sthash.yWNdj2KA.dpuf

http://www.latimes.com/opinion/opinion-la/la-ol-legalize-marijuana-free-prior-offenders-20140115,0,3562757.story#ixzz2qiYJD1dU

CHAPTER FIVE:

http://www.cmcr.ucsd.edu/

http://www.cancer.gov/cancertopics/pdq/cam/cannabis/patient/page1

http://azmedtest.com/educate/cannabinoids/

http://www.sacbee.com/2012/07/12/4625608/california-pot-research-backs.html#storylink=cpy

CHAPTER SIX:

Books

Green, G. (2010). *The cannabis grow bible: The definitive guide to growing marijuana for recreational and medical use.* San Francisco, Calif: Green Candy Press.

Websites

http://www.hightimes.com/read/breaking-down-medicinal-value-sativas

http://www.thcdigest.com/indica-vs-sativa/

http://patientsmarijuana.org/Sativa_or_Indica.html

http://www.medicaljane.com/2013/06/28/cannabis-indica-vs-cannabis-sativa-differences/#

www.leafly.com/hybrid/girl-scout-cookie

CHAPTER SEVEN:

Books

Schlosser, E. (2004). *Reefer madness: Sex, drugs, and cheap labor in the American black market.* Boston: Houghton Mifflin.

Websites

http://www.rollingstone.com/politics/pages/the-weed-issue-marijuana-legalization-status-by-state-weedmap-20130610

http://nation.time.com/2013/05/28/how-america-learned-to-stop-worrying-and-love-marijuana/

http://www.latimes.com/opinion/opinion-la/la-ol-legalize-marijuana-free-prior-offenders-20140115,0,3562757.story#ixzz2qiYYXKok

- http://www.drugwarfacts.org/cms/Crime#Total

- http://www.takepart.com/article/2013/01/02/no-relief-convicted

CHAPTER EIGHT:

http://marijuana-uses.com/learn/

http://rxmarijuana.com/wonder_drug.htm

http://norml.org/about/item/lester-grinspoon-md

http://rxmarijuana.com/marijuana_heretostay.htm

CHAPTER NINE:

- http://www.leap.cc/about/why-legalize-drugs/

- http://www.leap.cc/about/vision-mission/

-
http://www.pbs.org/wgbh/pages/frontline/shows/dope/etc/cron.html

- http://nation.time.com/2013/05/28/how-america-learned-to-stop-worrying-and-love-marijuana/

- http://www.kpbs.org/news/2010/oct/07/odd-history-marijuana-us/

ABOUT THE COVER DESIGN

The cover of *Cannabis Sense 2015* was created by the insanely talented Chris Keal, a terrific friend and one of the most brilliant creative thinkers our planet has ever known.

You can learn more about Mr. Keal's unparalleled graphic design skills at ChrisKeal.com or follow @ChrisKeal.

About the Author

Derek Williams is a graduate of Shippensburg University (B.A., '94) and the University of Tennessee (M.S., '95). He grew up in Lancaster County, Pennsylvania but is definitely not Amish.

Mr. Williams has lived in New York, Los Angeles, San Francisco, Austin, Philadelphia, Phoenix, Knoxville, Nebraska, Connecticut and New Jersey. He moved to Colorado in 2014 and is a registered medical marijuana patient.

Derek has smoked weed with Woody Harrelson at his house in the Hollywood Hills, been an extra in the movie *The Great Buck Howard* with John Malkovich and babysat Lady Gaga's fiancée Taylor Kinney like twenty times over a two year period in the late 1980s. He is the author of eight books on football, music and cannabis.

Contact the author:

> **email**: derekdwilliams@gmail.com

> **phone**: (720) 724-5533

> **web**: CannabisSenseAmerica.com

Also by Derek Williams (available on Amazon):

The Greatest College Football Quotes of All-Time

A Short History of Pink Floyd

Life Lessons, Wisdom & Advice from Legendary College Football Coaches

The Best College Football Quotes From Down South

The Most Hilarious Quotes, Quips, Insults and Zingers in College Football History

The Greatest Alabama Crimson Tide Football and Coach Paul "Bear" Bryant Quotes of All-Time

DEDICATION

This book is dedicated to Jack Herer, William O'Shaughnessy, Ed Rosenthal, Peter McWilliams, Lester Grinspoon, Tod H. Mikuriya, Charles Lynch, Carl Sagan and the memory of my uncle Bill Duffy.

A huge 'Thank You' goes out to Chris Keal for designing the (absolutely brilliant) cover of *Cannabis Sense*. If the Olympics handed out gold medals for 'Coolest Cat on Earth', my homeboy Keal would have more medallions around his neck than Michael Phelps.

www.ingramcontent.com/pod-product-compliance
Lightning Source LLC
Chambersburg PA
CBHW070143290526

45789CB00002B/607